Billy Connolly

The authorized version

Duncan Campbell is News Editor of *Time Out*.
While researching this book he spent three
months on tour with Billy Connolly.

Billy Connolly

The authorized version

compiled and with an introduction by DUNCAN CAMPBELL

A Pan original Pan Books

First published 1976 by Pan Books Ltd,
Cavaye Place, London SW10 9PG
ISBN O 330 24767 0
extracts from Billy Connolly's stage routines
© Billy Connolly 1976
Introduction and other text © Pan Books Ltd 1976
Printed and bound in Great Britain by
Hazell Watson & Viney Ltd,
Aylesbury, Bucks

Contents

Odiously Rude, Offensive & Lavatorial Stuff
McGlumpher the Lavvie Attendant, Chanty Techniques &
If God had meant us to fart he would have given us a
funnel 185

6

Acknowledgements

Wee Billy
Frank
George
Jan
Iris
Brian
Robin
Davie
Miles
and
Sam Glove

Introduction

At five past eleven on the night of Tuesday, 21 October 1975, in the ABC cinema, Belfast, a slim dark-haired Irish girl in a white blouse ran up to the stage from the auditorium with a rose in her hand.

In the audience were the Chief of Staff of the Official IRA in the North, the chairman of the Protestant Action Group, a leading member of the Provisional IRA, a Unionist MP, the Public Relations man for Long Kesh Internment Camp, two flak-jacketed soldiers with rifles in one hand and ready-to-be-autographed photos in the other, eighteen off-duty policemen and warders with Chicagoan bulges under their arms, and nearly two thousand Belfast citizens on a night out.

The girl attracted the attention of the man standing alone on the stage dressed in a pair of black tights, black leotard and yellow, banana-shaped Wellington boots.

She handed him the rose. He thanked her and moved back to put it down on the chair where his Ode banjo was resting. Just before he reached the chair, he sniffed the rose and – BOOOOM! – imitated the sound of an exploding bomb. The audience burst into laughter and applause. And Billy Connolly saluted the last night of his longest, most successful and prestigious tour.

'Thank you, Belfast – you were amazin',' he said, waving the rose and a bottle of Irn Bru at the standing ovation below him.

'Aye, so are you, Big Yin,' said a tall, grey-haired Irishman in the balcony, almost to himself.

The final night of the 1975 tour was a peak in the long series of show-business mountaineering expeditions that Billy had begun back in 1966, when he quit his job as a welder on the Clyde to try and make it as a singer and performer.

Five years with his banjo and guitar in Scottish folk clubs, London pubs, Amsterdam halls and Danish beer-gardens followed. Then, in 1971, he parted company with the Humblebums, the fourth group he had been playing with, went solo and became an overnight flop in a one-man show in Musselburgh.

But then came the Great Northern Welly Boot Show which curled the hair of the Edinburgh Festival Fringe, and since then the climbing has never really stopped: gold albums, a Number One hit record, a packed London Palladium one-nighter, Parkinson shows, a record-breaking fortnight at the Glasgow Apollo centre, a ticket-tout's spree at London's New Victoria and a stack of 'We-could-make-you-big-in-America-Australia-Tibet' offers when he returned from the 1975 tour to his 'villa' on Loch Lomondside.

To describe Billy Connolly as a Scottish comedian is a bit like calling Hannibal a Carthaginian elephant-driver. So dozens of journalists, critics and fans have battled with each other for the aptest comparisons to draw. He is 'like Lenny Bruce', a description that bores Billy now almost as much as a civic reception; an 'electric Harry Lauder', 'Scot of the Anarchic', 'as good as the young Eric Morecambe and Marty Feldman', 'Partick's answer to Chaucer'; he has 'a bit of Max Miller in him'; and he 'touches the heights of Pablo Picasso, Buster Keaton, George Best, W. S. Gilbert'.

Physically, he has become another 'Merlin the Magician', he's like a 'tartan Frank Zappa', 'a Hell's Angel with a sense of humour', and 'the man who got the last haircut in the shop'.

The Book of Scottish Clichés has been rifled to describe his impact: 'the best thing to come out of Scotland since Scotch whisky', 'the funniest since Bonnie Prince Charlie in drag', 'the most valuable since North Sea oil', 'Glesgae belongs to him'. His six-year-old son Jamie told his class at school that his Dad 'plays the guitar and sings about jobbies'.

A wander through the streets of Glasgow turns into a procession of grinning followers anxious to shake a hand, slap a back, tell a joke or cajole an autograph on the back of a bus-ticket or a cigarette packet. Windows are thrown open, nicotined fingers beckon into pub doorways, little snot-nosed children are held up to see 'The Big Yin' – The Big One, – a title given unconditionally by a country that usually keeps its heroes on a football pitch or in a patriot's grave.

An Indian waiter, bringing out Billy's take-away chicken Madras in one of Glasgow's 'Curry Valley' restaurants, writes, 'For the Big Yin, Nae Bother' on the top of the silverfoil container and slips half a dozen Tennant's lagers into the bag since it's after closing time. A fan sends round a pair of wellies delicately wrapped in a pink ribbon for the opening night in London. A Greenock sculptor welds a three foot-high caricature for his Drymen sitting-room. And when he pans English sausages on the Michael Parkinson show, a dozen worried sausage manufacturers bombard him with samples.

Born in Anderston on the 24th of November, 1942, to William and Mary – 'No' a bad combination of names, eh?' – Billy came from the sort of background that still provides the west of Scotland with the guts of its industrial workforce.

The people he grew up with work in the shipyards, as welders or platers or 'sparks', or go to sea, or drive lorries or serve their time in the Army or in jail. They support Glasgow Celtic or Partick Thistle, drink in the pubs at night, perhaps go to Spain or Majorca for their holidays, though their parents would have taken them to Rothesay, read the *Daily Record* and vote Labour.

His father was a Post Office technician. His mother left home when he was five; he didn't see her again until he was thirty. He was performing at the Ashfield Club in Glasgow when a middle-aged woman came backstage to ask if he was Billy Connolly.

'I thought she wanted an autograph . . . then she said, "I think I'm your mother." There's no answer to that. So I bought her a drink.'

Aunts and William Connolly senior brought Billy up and sent him off to school – greetin' – in Partick. His sister Flo, two years older, is now a teacher herself. Michael, his younger brother, is a postman.

In 1956, the family moved to Drumchapel – 'the desert wi' windaes' – but Mr Connolly now lives back in Partick, next door to Billy's aunt.

After Billy left school, he embarked on a few of the jobs available to a 15-year-old Glasgow boy with not too many exam qualifications and no great desire to join the Army in the year after Suez. He became a bookshop messenger boy, was sacked, and delivered bread before starting his apprenticeship in Stephens' shipyard on the Clyde.

The eight years he spent in the yards fuelled him with material for the future, but also became a kind of albatross round his neck: 'Billy Connolly – isn't he the one who was a docker? No? Oh, a welder – yes I knew it was something like that.' He acknowledges his debt to the yards but tires of constant questions about it . . . 'Gi'es a break. I've been out of it for as long as I was in it.'

In the meantime he had joined the Territorial Army and learnt how to parachute. He clocked up seventeen jumps and came out of it all with a fine, a reprimand and a kitbag full of juicy reminiscences.

He had also been to Biafra, working on an oil rig in Port Harcourt while the war was hotting up, before he was encouraged by friends at the yards to do something more with his banjo and guitar playing . . . 'I got one of those "Learn-in-a-Day" guitar books . . . you know, "Impress your Friends, Be Invited to Trendy Parties." They didnae tell you you had to bring a carry-oot as well . . .'

After a nervous start as a solo act, he joined a group with his banjo teacher, moved into the forgettable Skillet-Lickers and on to the Acme Brush Company, before finding a small slice of success with Tam Harvey, and later with Gerry Rafferty, in the Humblebums.

By now he had met his wife, Iris Pressagh, a good-looking, dark-haired interior decorator, at a Polish Club in Glasgow, where he was playing. 'My initials are WC and hers are IP – there must be something in that.' They now live at their fourteenth address since they got married, in Drymen, Stirlingshire, with their two children, Jamie and two-year-old Cara, two labradors, a hamster, a rabbit, a squatting owl and a deaf white cat called Doughball.

It was when Gerry Rafferty went off to form Stealer's Wheel that Billy tried to make it alone, stumbled about for a while and finally came across what he really wanted to do full time: make people laugh.

While he was still with the Humblebums, the gift was already becoming apparent: he won more response from his between-song chat than he did from his banjo and guitar playing, which he has never been overly proud of anyway. In any case, he found himself under the musical shadow of Rafferty, whose unrealized potential is a constant source of late-night frustration to Billy. For Billy, the idea of someone *not* becoming a star when they could seems almost heresy.

But the idea of Billy actually *being* a star is near-heresy to quite a large body of people in Scotland. After he did a Glasgow translation of the story of Moses – 'So the bush says tae Moses, "Nip hame and get yer peepil"' – for the BBC religious affairs programme in Scotland, a

13

demonstration, headed by militant Protestant Pastor Jack Glass, was mounted outside the Kelvin Hall studios . . . 'Ah, well, it's no' every day you get a demonstration in your honour.'

His most famous/notorious routine, about the Last Supper as it took place in Gallowgate, Glasgow, rather than Galilee, brought howls of protest from a Scotland still with John Knox in its closet. But many churchmen loved it.

The album on which that piece appears, *Solo Concert*, has now sold more than a quarter of a million copies. His previous solo album, also on Transatlantic, has sold well into six figures. And all this despite the fact that, to the majority of people south of Dumfries, the notion of buying a Scottish comedian's album was about as enticing as investing in a volume of Icelandic Love Poems.

When Polydor, his current record company, brought out *Cop Yer Whack for This* – a phrase that loosely translated into English means 'Take this, you bounder' – the climate was beginning to change. In Scotland he was already a legend, but the album, the Parkinson show, a profile by George Rosie in the Sunday Times magazine and the Palladium appearance confirmed his presence in the south.

Soon Billy became a kind of Clydeside Shrine of Lourdes, visited by politicians and journalists and film makers and tour promoters and TV front-men, who *knew* that just a touch of the hem of the polka-dotted flares would heal them. Harold Wilson met him in Glasgow and was captured in a beautiful photo beside him, white heather in buttonhole and hands folded quietly as if in prayer. Willie Ross, the Labour Secretary of State for Scotland, went to see his show in Edinburgh. Billy made a broadcast for the Labour Party in the 1974 election and drove through the night to help in the campaign of Labour candidate Brian Wilson in Ross-shire; Billy had known Brian, then the editor of the *West Highland Free Press*, since the days when the latter was a precocious concert promoter. Willie Ormond, the Scottish football team manager, asked Billy over to Munich for the 1974 World Cup to help raise the sagging spirits of another of Scotland's wayward national obsessions.

A cartoon strip called 'The Big Yin', which Billy writes with cartoonist Malcolm McCormick, himself a musician with the Vindscreen Vipers skiffle group, appeared in the *Sunday Mail* to change Scottish Sunday breakfast reading patterns for the first time since the *Sunday Post* gave birth to 'The Broons and Oor Wullie'. In one classic episode, 'Billy's uncle' comes down from Uist and is told 'If yir jist gauny sit scroungin' bevvy, ye can away back wheer the animals roam aboot an' streams run dooni slopes.' – 'Ye mean Hampden!'

When the big 1975 tour got under way, it was garlanded with Big Yin posters, T-shirts, postcards, colour slides, key-rings, Nippie Sweeties and welly-shaped candles (The T-shirt, it was discovered by Miles, the man responsible for selling them, could, by moving the belly backwards and forwards, make Billy's face appear to be in mid-vomit.)

During the course of the eight-week tour, a single record, 'D-I-V-O-R-C-E', a parody of Tammy Wynette, – 'I always thought she was Roy Rogers in drag' – had hit the streets, and an album, *Get Right Intae Him* had been completed. 'D-I-V-O-R-C-E' made its way to number one within a month: disc jockey Tony Blackburn told his audience of housewives that he had played it seven times and still couldn't see anything funny about it; perhaps one of the highest recommendations a comedy record can get!

The tour itself was constantly invaded by 'the greats and the near-greats', squeezing into the dressing-room to sample the free champagne and food – 'Hey, get your haunds off those grapes, they're mine!' In Aberdeen, the local football team came round after the show and were treated to a performance that must have made getting up in the morning for training virtually impossible.

A hopeful fan pushed a joke under the stage door before the show started: 'I've got a job circumcising elephants; the pay's bad, but the tips are enormous.' 'Jesus Christ, does he expect me to use *that*?'

In Glasgow, Bay City Roller Les McKeown took a night off from being mobbed to bring round a BCR watch and BCR platform shoes. Miss Great Britain, Susan Cuff, in Scotland to promote milk, was whisked along to the show.

'I've heard so much about you,' she said to a puzzled Davie Craig, the other half of High Speed Grass, when she was taken backstage. 'No' me, no' me . . .' And she was introduced to Billy. 'Imagine a name like that – Sue Cuff – see what it sounds like in Scottish.'

Max Bygraves and Bryan Ferry sent regards when he arrived at the New Victoria in London. Vanessa Redgrave, shortly after the police raid on her Worker's Revolutionary Party headquarters, came backstage. And the arrival of the Dubliners and Nazareth together sent ripples up the spines of the New Vic bouncers.

Alex Harvey, another of Glasgow's favourite sons, entertained the first-night party with a long explanation of the fact that only two non-Red Indians had ever been made Indian chiefs: men called, inevitably, McLintock and McCormick. On the last night, it was David Essex and the 'celebs' at the Hilton . . . 'As I was sayin' to Twiggy, "the nights are fair drawin' in".'

The adulation in London was not entirely unexpected. But it was ironic that it should have come at a time when the Scottish press were beginning to feel that Billy had got too big for his wellies.

This feeling had originated in 1974 when the press made much of the fact that Billy had walked off stage in Aviemore because of a hostile audience reaction, and had simmered through the winter. Not that the reaction was entirely unexpected, particularly since Billy is neither discreet nor ostentatiously modest. There is an old Scottish joke about the Second Coming. A man rushes down the street to tell his neighbours:

'He's here! He's here! He's come!'
'Who has?'
'Jesus Christ!'
'Aye . . . I kent his faither.'

And it was this feeling that Billy was, after all, nothing special, certainly no guru, and that too much fuss was being made, that surfaced in the press.

Billy's detractors come in three main categories: there are the 'I-kent-his-faither's, who explain that there are hundreds of people in Glasgow pubs with just the same gift for patter and joke-telling; Connolly is 'just lucky and has a pushy manager'.

17

Then there are the ones who find his humour 'lavatorial and offensive', such as Donald Bruce of the *Daily Record*: 'There is a borderline between the screamingly funny and the odiously rude. Unfortunately, Billy crossed that line.' Others let him know about it anonymously or through the readers' letters columns: 'I'm sure Connolly only caters to a minute section of Scotland,' wrote Mrs Miller from Edinburgh to the *Record*. 'But, of course, where there's muck, there's brass.'

But perhaps the most critical of all are the 'folkies', who knew Billy in folk club days and cannot quite take the Name in Lights, the massive cut-out figure bestriding the Apollo in Renfield Street, the sixteen-piece orchestra and the TV shows. They just want Billy to 'come home' to where he's really appreciated – the folk clubs and pubs of Scotland.

Billy's ultimate departure from that circuit was partly due to the astuteness of agent Eddie Tobin, who spotted him at the Traverse Tattoo in Edinburgh, a sort of trailer for the Edinburgh Festival. Tobin is now a member of Unicorn Artists, the organization headed by 36-year-old Frank Lynch.

Frank saw Billy perform for the first time in the White Elephant in Edinburgh, slapped his thigh, bit the carpet and arranged for a meeting the next day. Since then he has watched from the wings as Billy takes ovation after ovation, drinking pineapple juice at the receptions and looking on as the London wheeler-dealers express their amazement that such a thoroughbred success should come out of a Glasgow stable.

But Frank remains discreetly in the background now, leaving the day-to-day hustling to Billy's personal manager or handler or super-roadie or whatever you call the person who has to drive the lime-yellow Mercedes station wagon, pacify the press, comfort the groupies, wake the Man at ten after he has gone to bed at nine, keep an eye on the wellies, find the finger-picks, wrap the banjo in its Glasgow Corporation towel, lock the Guild guitar into its denim-covered case, order the champagne and smile inscrutably when strangers ask 'But what's he *really* like?'

28-year-old George Miller was Billy's first full-time roadie and moved into that profession's Saloon Bar of Fame when Billy recorded a track entitled 'George, my Faithful Roadie', which immortalized the fact that George's head had been put on upside down – Viking beard below and bald on top. By 1975, George had become tour manager, still aggressively loyal; when the *Telegraph* in Dundee called Billy's act 'uninspired and uninspiring', he set fire to the paper on the Caird Hall stage. 'You're worse than the bloody kids at the Slade concerts,' said the janitor, stamping out the flames.

George, who used to be a civil servant with the Department of Health and Social Security, now found himself running a tour that was to be seen by more than 140,000 people. He celebrated the start of it in Holburn Street, Aberdeen: the Interflora shop there had a poster of Sir Winston Churchill in its window, captioned: *A Great Statesman. Would that we had one like him today*. George and accomplice drove there in the middle of the night to slap up a poster of rock singer Roy Wood on top of Sir Winston and add the line: *We have.*

The present roadie-handler-factotum is 31-year-old Billy Johnstone, 'The Wee Yin', a short dark-haired man who, with his dark glasses on, looks like Dustin Hoffman as Ratso Rizzo in *Midnight Cowboy*.

The two met when Billy J. was a 'spark' in the same shipyard as Billy C. 'I'd seen him in the Marland Bar and noticed him because there weren't that many hairy guys around at the time. Then I saw him in the yards so I said: "I saw you at the Marland Bar, didn't I?" And he said "What about it?"'

Subsequently Billy Johnstone went north, working on the Glencoe ski-lift – 'I have to lie on the floor of the car as we go through; I owe money still' – and running a hot-dog stand, with some unasked-for promotional help from Billy.

He drove the Humblebums for a while but was out of work when Billy asked him if he fancied joining him: 'It's changed now; we don't sleep on the floors any more.' He, too, had a brief spell performing as a singer with the Roving Journeymen, and, as far as some of the Glencoe people are concerned, is as funny as Connolly.

Often he can be. 'Trendy Bill frae Maryhill' – he still lives there, in 'the Barracks' – has one brilliant routine about a famous Scottish comedian who is a 'secret junkie' and has been trapped in a club by the police, who want him to take his kilt jacket off so that they can look at his arms. And he can rattle off the patter to keep at bay the people who approach him as a way of reaching Connolly, or diverting the aggressive drunk in the hotel late at night while Billy C. is trying to attract the night porter's attention by shouting 'NURSE!'

When the choice was made for a supporting act to go on the 1975 tour, Billy was adamant that two old friends, Robin

McKidd and Davie Craig of High Speed Grass, should come with him; they introduced themselves as 'the band that put the count in country music, 1–2–3–4 . . .'

The three of them had known each other for eight or nine years and Robin and Davie had organized a small and memorably unsuccessful tour of Scottish holiday resorts that Billy had been on when he first went solo.

Davie, with a face that looks as though it has had a brief but passionate affair with a broken bottle, came from a family where the father played Scottish country violin, the mother classical violin, the three sons the bagpipes and the three daughters the piano. He had bumped into Billy periodically over the years while they were playing in the same sort of clubs and had yet to see him go down badly with an audience. Davie meanwhile was filling-in between his music work with jobs as a sugar beet factory-worker, fisherman, labourer, Customs and Excise man, paper mill worker, British Steel Corporation clerk and all the other forms of employment necessary for anyone hoping to sing the Fife blues.

Robin, the cadaverous one, found himself returning to play to packed houses in a London that he had left after working there as a caviare salesman in Soho, a van-driver in Mayfair and a removal man in Hampstead. He had played the circuit in Scotland, taught guitar at the local school, and had watched a near-riot when Billy first started making it and played a tiny Perth hall with a capacity of 150 and a punter potential of three times the number.

In London the two of them found themselves being driven back to their hotel from Dingwalls' Dance-Hall in Billy's chauffeured Rolls Royce . . .

'There was a tramp,' said Robin, 'who saw a Rolls stop at the traffic lights and went up to it and tapped on the window to ask for some money. The man inside rolled down his window and said: "Neither a borrower nor a lender be – Shakespeare." Then he rolled the window up and the car drove off. At the next traffic lights the tramp caught it up again. He tapped on the window and the man rolled it down. "Cunt – DH Lawrence," said the tramp.'

It was almost as though it was as important for Billy to have wee Billy, George, Robin and Davie with him on tour as it was for Muhammad Ali to have Angelo Dundee and Bundini Brown with him in Manila. (Billy drove to Leicester in the middle of the tour to watch the Ali–Frazier fight on closed-circuit TV, and accorded Ali his own standing ovation at the end.) With all the madness, the adulation, the offers, the gushings, the wet-eyed appreciation and the reception-crawling, he knew there was always a familiar Scoto-cynical eye to catch.

In Troon, where he had his first pint ever– 'I'd been on whisky since I was twelve, but that was my first pint' – he popped into the pub to check it out fourteen years later.

'You're no' Billy Connolly,' said a delighted big woman. 'You're much better-lookin' than he is!'

Down the street, at the fish shop, following the sign that says 'Carry Out Round the Corner', the little dumpling behind the serving-hatch is struck dumb.

'Three fish suppers wi' Ukrainian salt . . . and if you've no' got any, make it Siberian. OK? Christ, it's such a problem that . . . gettin' vinegar on the steering-wheel of your Mercedes.'

An old man in Connelly's bar, opposite John Brown's shipyards, wants Billy to come back to his house, because otherwise his son will never believe he has met him. Fine. But before the visit, the old man insists on buying a round: 'I've got enough money to last me a lifetime, Billy – if I die tomorrow.'

The police are also frequent visitors to the shows and come round afterwards, their uniforms taking them where the autograph hunters cannot roam. Billy sees one coming into the Usher Hall dressing-room in Edinburgh and takes off his ring before he shakes hands with him.

'Hey,' he says to two policewomen in Dundee, 'fancy comin' along to the show and bookin' me for obscenity? Make me feel like Lenny Bruce.'

Opening a store in Paisley, Billy finds himself surrounded by policemen preparing to have a group photo of themselves taken with him. Meanwhile, someone has casually stolen a large roll of carpet from inside and quietly driven off with it . . .

The Mercedes pulls in at a petrol station on the way from Aberdeen to Glasgow. It is a Sunday and Billy has already been shocked to see young men playing football on the Sabbath – 'and I wouldnae be surprised if they go into a hotel afterwards and drink alcohol . . . terrible.'

The woolly-hatted petrol-pump attendant spots Billy getting out to buy some Coke.

'Hey, Big Yin, gi'es two free tickets!'

'Aye,' says Billy, 'here's two. For Preston.'

Further south, just before the Forth Road bridge crosses into Edinburgh, another garage proprietor recognizes him and wants to let everyone know of his discovery. First he points Billy out to all his other customers, then runs off to find his wife.

'We've been married thirty-one years, Billy,' he explains as he hurries back with her.

'Serves you right.'

Others are almost as aware of the Name. In the Angus Hotel in Dundee, Billy was settling down to a late-night cold ham and chips and a discussion of Patty Hearst, who had been captured that morning.

'You're full of shit,' said a voice from the far side of the room.

'Oh, aye . . .'

A small, natty figure in a denim suit and American accent introduces himself; he has left Glasgow and found fortune in America as a computer salesman. He wants to explain to the assembled scruffs how they could better themselves in the same way. Finally, detecting a lack of interest, he confides:

'Billy O'Connell, the Scots comedian,' he says, with the fascinated Billy sitting in the next swivel chair down, 'is staying *in this hotel*.'

'Naw! Really?'

'Could you get us tickets for him?' asks George. 'I'd love to see him close up.'

'Sure,' says denim suit, 'I'll fix it on my expense account.'

'What's he like, though?' pursues George.

'Oh, just typical Glasgow comic . . . the red nose . . . the bow-tie . . . half-Jewish . . .'

Dundee was perhaps the low-watermark of the tour, the one place where the hall was not sold out and where the papers managed the most lukewarm of receptions; for D.C. Thomson, the local press barons, seemed to find Connolly offensive.

It was in Dundee that the nastiest anonymous letter arrived, and it was here that two fans tried to grab Billy for an autograph, just as he was about to go on stage. He refused and they waited behind afterwards to catcall him.

'Oh, look at the great Billy Connolly . . . thanks *very* much for your autograph . . .'

Billy gazed at them in bewilderment, like a chartered accountant accused of rape by a strange woman at a bus stop. 'What the hell's she on about?'

A common view of Billy is of a massively heavy drinker, the sort of performer who needs intravenous caffeine injections before he is poured on stage by a manager who quietly prays in the wings that he won't throw up over the front stalls.

But he has a Cup of Tea before he goes on. Which is a bit like discovering that Mick Jagger spends his most debauched evenings watching The Generation Game on TV. ('That Mick Jagger – when he was a wain, his mother would take him shopping, lick his lips and stick him to the windae of the supermarket so that he wouldnae get lost.')

Not that this discourages the bevvyed hordes from flocking to see him: one was sick on top of two old ladies at the Apollo, prompting the suggestion that he should be incorporated into the tour to add realism to the routine about the 'rubber men' waiting for the last bus to Drumchapel: 'Aye, you would just hear them shoutin' on Hughie, and the whole bus would lift their feet up.'

And there were plenty of them at the other concerts, too. Frank Lynch disposed of one at the New Victoria in London. He returned to tell Frank 'I'll come back and *get* ye!'

'This man,' said Frank to an intervening London policeman, 'is a *real ned*.'

'I'm sorry, sir,' said the policeman. 'I don't understand you.'

'Aye,' said Frank, 'but *he* does.'

Billy makes up for the abstinence after the show, when pints of heavy are sunk like German U-boats in the kind of old war movie that he loves to parody . . . 'Roger didn't have to go back . . . but he wanted to save Charles . . . I'm afraid he must have bought it over the drink . . . ran into the Jerries on his way home . . .'

Sometimes the night before makes itself obvious on the morning after: 'Aye, you don't get eyes like that frae playin' table tennis . . . ma head feels like *mince*.'

When the tour reached Dublin, it was joined by a film crew, headed by Murray Grigor who had directed *Clydeoscope*, the film in which Billy plays the first man to come up the Clyde – on a bicycle. The crew filmed his every move (almost), even being on hand to record 'Billy Connolly Getting Out of Bed After Three Hours' Sleep'.

'We didn't get one of him being sick, though,' said one of them wryly.

When Billy arrived at Heathrow airport en route for Dublin he was still white with weariness and nerves, but smiling. Checking out the private 'jetliner' that was to fly the party to Ireland, he spotted the modest eight-seater Piper Navaho.

'Well, I feel a little less like Hugh Hefner and a little more like Amelia Erhardt . . . Christ, see what it says on the wing – "Buddy Holly Airlines".'

'Nice way to travel,' says the uniformed man on the desk looking at the bleary long-haired party.

'What he means,' says Billy, 'is "Nice way for scruff like you to travel" . . . he can't understand how a bunch of windae-cleaners are travelling in a private plane.'

Once inside the plane, with 'Biggles', the bearded pilot, apologizing for the clogged runway, Billy Johnstone asks if the firm, Logan Air, was owned by Jimmy Logan.

'Naw – he hires bikes at Millport.'

Dublin predictably laid on the noisiest and booziest 'press conference', although whether the 150 people crowding into the room at the Gresham Hotel were all representatives of the media is debatable. It was decided that the ones who asked where the bar was were the bona fide press and the ones who asked where Billy was were not.

The Carlton cinema was packed to the gills, with hundreds standing down the aisles, ready and well-oiled for Billy when he appeared around midnight.

'I-R-A!' shouted a voice in the middle of one of his early numbers.

'Aye, you're very brave down there in the dark, pal. Try shoutin' that in the middle of Ibrox Park sometime. . .'

Throughout the tour there had been slight changes in the act as it headed further south. 'Chanty' and 'semmit' were translated, 'shite' became 'shit' and 'wain' was sometimes 'kid'. Also, for some reason, Ivan the Terrible, the wrestler in one of Billy's stories, had been carrying a half-eaten baby in his hand as far as Scottish audiences were concerned; in London he made do with a dog.

Belfast had become the sort of tour bogey, the Full Stop, a date loaded with macabre jokes: 'Oh, you'll go down a bomb in Belfast, Billy . . . That's where the tour ends, is it? Very good . . .' Billy Johnstone was briefing the tour party on who was to be rear-gunner in the plane flying in.

There was some reason for the paranoia. It was not unknown that Billy was, by birth if by nothing else, a Catholic and that he made cracks about Orangemen (and bigoted Catholics, too, but somehow those never quite got the same publicity). Also the recent massacre of the Miami Showband had not boosted people's confidence about performing in Ulster.

Johnny Cash had just cancelled his proposed visit at the last minute. 'He plays at being the haard maan,' said one of the bouncers at the ABC in Belfast, ' – he's about as haard as a butter scone.' The previous night, Billy, never a man for half-measures, had had a dream about Abraham Lincoln.

At the door of the ABC, everyone was searched as usual but there was no sign of the Ring-of-Steel, snipers-on-the-rooftop, usherettes-in-bullet-proof-pinafores that had been darkly predicted.

'I don't know why there's any reason to feel nervous,' said a Belfast woman journalist to Billy in his dressing-room between shows. 'It's as safe here as it is in Manchester or Birmingham.'

'Aye . . . but my name's Billy Connolly, no' Johnny Weissmuller.'

The audience loved the show, and their final standing ovation ranked beside the other happiest reactions of the tour: the man falling downstairs in Aberdeen because he couldn't stand the pain of laughing any more; the women who threw Billy two smokies from the balcony in Dundee; the Birmingham fan, a screwtop-hardened heavy, who wept on Billy's shoulder; the tiny porter in the hotel in Birmingham who wanted to carry all of Billy's instruments: 'He used to be in the Marines, lied about his height.'

Then it was away to the airport, running towards the small planes that were to take film crew and the rest of the tour back to Scotland – 'Last one tae Glasgow's a poof!' Biggles handed Frank Lynch his ice-pick to open the bottles and took off as Billy launched into an imitation of Ian Paisley having just seen the show: 'Sure, the boy's got a lot of taalent – for a Papist.'

Back in Glasgow, a welcome-home party in the dressing-room of the Apollo, with Billy Johnstone, champagne glass in one hand, fat cigar in the other, doing a soft-shoe shuffle and singing:

As I walk along the Maryhill Road
With an independent air,
You can hear the folk declare
'He must be a millionaire –
He's the man who broke the bank at Kinlochleven!'

The rest of this book is a collection of various patterings of Billy on subjects near to and far from his heart: drunks and football and jiving and jobbies and Margaret Thatcher and Durex and prisons and batterings and piranhas and Mary Queen of Scots and the Big Sui and willies and unions and fly-men and bevvy and the Scotia Bar and America and judges and the Cubs and Biafran nights and the police and middens and hymns. They are a collection of late-night rambles, sensible mid-afternoon interviews, on-stage patter and closing time stories.

Probably the best way to read them is just after playing a Billy Connolly album. If that is not possible, and the reader has never been to Glasgow, the next best way is to phone up a Glasgow number at random (just dial 041, then any seven numbers) and listen to the accent at the other end until the pips go.

Duncan Campbell
December 1975

Billy Connolly

Born Anderston, Scotland. 24th November, 1942
Weight Variable from 12 stone 4 pounds to 12 stone 14
pounds
Height 7 foot 2 inches
Nickname Big Yin (Big One). (See above)
Married Iris Pressagh, 1968
Children Son, Jamie, born 1969; daughter, Cara, born 1973
Education St Peter's Primary School; St Gerard's
Favourite food Curried smarties, figs
Favourite drink Yes
Influences Scottish and Newcastle
Home Drymen, Stirlingshire
Discography
Billy Connolly Live (Transatlantic TRA 258)
Solo Concert (Transatlantic TRA 279)
Words and Music (Transatlantic TRA SAM 32)
Cop Yer Whack for This (Polydor 2383310)
Get Right Intae Him (Polydor 2383368)
Hobbies Fishing, Tibet, fishing in Tibet
Ambitions To go to Agatha Christie's front door, ring the
bell, wait for the butler to answer it, then shout '*You* did it!'

SCHOOLDAYS The Lucky Midden, Crossing the Big Sui & the Peewit Patrol

It's funny, now that I'm a bit famous, I bump into my old teachers and they always say, 'We're very proud of you, Connolly. I always knew you would do well. You were always one of my favourite pupils.' So how come they were always battering me?

I was back at my wee school, my primary school, St Peter's, to do something for BBC Nationwide and it was all so changed. I was amazed at how good it was in comparison to when I was there. The classrooms all used to be painted in this horrible Glasgow Corporation pastel green, but now it's all white and nice and warm.

The great enormous crucifix has gone and the teachers are all young and gay, in the sense of what the word used to mean; nothing like the pterodactyls that we used to have.

All that stuff they give you about your schooldays being the happiest of your life is just a load of rubbish. The teachers I had were a load of psychopaths. And the janitor . . . always shopping you . . .

'Oh, aye, I saw him smoking behind the lavvie. That's the one!'

Cinnamon sticks they were. You couldn't keep them alight long enough to smoke them. One time he even came into the lavvie when we were all puffing away, got a light off us and then went and told the teacher!

And I was one of the unfortunates who lived in the same street as his school, so he could shop me in the holidays as well.

It was at St Peter's that I heard my first-ever joke. It was a kind of rhyme:

Pat and Mick
Went up a stick
And couldnae get down
For skelfs.

I thought it was hysterical. What it means, I'll never know, but it was my first joke and I was very proud of it. And they tell the same sort of jokes today. One of Jamie's wee pals was round at the house and told me one and it was just the same kind that we had when I was at school; they don't change at all.

Of course, I got lots of material from my schooldays: all the snotters and peeing in my pants and the lying that went on about the size of people's willies.

Archie Mackenzie, the guy who could fart in stereo is just a figment of my imagination, though. But the piece I do about strange names came from an actual guy I knew called Constantine O'Brien. Which was unfortunate, because by the time I did the piece he had changed his name by deed poll to Stan. Then when I did the record, everyone knew that it was him and started calling him Constantine again. It's a bit heavy; if I'd known that he'd done that, I'd have chosen a different name, made one up.

I learnt how to insult people then, too. The worst you could call someone was 'smelly.' Or you would say 'Your ma's a darkie.' When I first came across swearing, I thought it was a great thing to do so I swore like a trooper for ages. In one sentence I would put in every swear-word I knew – and didn't have a clue what any of them meant. And I recall the delight when you got a dictionary and found out that 'bugger' was in it.

Some of my parody stuff was started at school, usually mimicking masters, particularly the ones with deformities. Most of the time it was a very cruel sort of humour.

I've never done much on deformities in my act. But in the playground at school, there was a wee spastic boy who had a short leg and a high boot and all the kids used to walk behind him in a big line, like a snake, imitating him. Everyone at school who had a deformity was laughed at from the moment they arrived until the moment they left. But it wasn't done in a mocking way; in fact, they were totally accepted. But we didn't say, 'Let's pretend he's the same.' That's silly.

At school itself I didn't get much of a chance to perform but there were all the Gang Shows, when I was in the Cubs and Scouts. And there were other things that Catholics have, like a priest having a Jubilee, just like the Queen, when he's been twenty-five years in the business, sort of thing. They would have a concert in their honour and give them a bung and I would get into that.

I was in the Cubs in Partick, the 141. I loved every second of it.

The Cubs are all arranged in Sixes and each Six has its different colour. I always wanted to be in the Red Six because they had a wee red triangle on the sleeve, like the

Bass Heavy ads. But I ended up in the Grey Six. I mean, God Almighty, who wants to be in the *Grey* Six?

Then when I joined the Scouts, I thought, At last I'm shot of the Grey Six. Now I'll be in a Patrol. They'll make me a Cobra or a Buffalo. Or a Wolf maybe. What bloody patrol did they put me in? The Peewits.

I got very few badges in the Scouts, didn't come up through the ranks at all. I had the stars and the swimming badge, but that was all. Then after I'd done the Tenderfoot, I chucked it.

In fact, I didn't like the Scouts at all. I think the best you can do is become a spastic and be presented to the Queen Mother at Balmoral; I think that's the highest accolade they have to offer. But I didn't distinguish myself much, just enjoyed the good times; which was much the same as in the Terris, where I stayed a private all the time and just had a ball.

We used to go off on expeditions with the Cubs – to bloody Milngavie. Are you ready for that? We would go in the tram and it would be magic. And to Busby. All these places that now seem so near, but at the time it was a great expedition.

I was involved in all the sport at school and loved the football. But I was rubbish – though the only prize I ever won was for the five-a-side football. They gave us a pair of *swimming trunks* as a prize. I don't go to the football very much now, there's too much bother; but I support Partick Thistle. They'll be in Europe next season. If there's a war on.

So I didn't shine at sport too much. In fact, I think my greatest sporting achievement was when I beat the North of England Darts Champion in a pub once. He was so angry about it he was almost in tears.

When I was still quite young, I had my own gang – THE CONNOLLYS – and we used to fight with The Sinclairs, who came from round the corner. We made tomahawks with tin cans and sticks: you bashed the can over a stick with a brick and made a sort of hatchet affair. And we would fill a tin can full of ashes, shove it in a nylon stocking, whirl it round our heads and hurl it into the enemy camp, leaving this big smokey trail behind it. I can't recall anyone being hurt, though there was a fair bit of walloping going on; but no slashing or anything like that.

There used to be these air-raid shelters all over the place and we would leap around on top of them. There was the 'Shelter-to-Shelter' jump, which was legendary. They were like mountaineering passes and routes: the White Patch, the Wee Sui and the Big Sui, which was short for suicide.

The Day I Jumped the Big Sui . . . oh, the feeling. It was like suddenly maturing, like the Indian brave's initiation rites, passing into manhood. And being able to jump the Big Sui was no mean feat. Maybe it was because I was a wee boy, but it seemed like one *hell* of a distance to jump. It was from the top of the air-raid shelter, across a void with railings in the middle of it that divided one back court from another, and then you had to land on top of this midden with a sloped roof. You had to stop dead there or you were right off over the other side.

Geordie Sinclair's attempt at it – what picturesque
memories I have of my childhood – I remember well.
Geordie was wearing these boots that a lot of the boys wore
at the time. Parish boots they were called; all studded and
tackety and funny. And he was running like a madman, like
a dervish, across the shelter, then leapt into the air and Did
the Big Sui. But when he hit the midden, he went into an
incredibly fast slide and ended up in mid-air in a sitting
position, with a trail of sparks coming from his studs.
Landed right on his arse in the back green.

Gerald McGee, who lived in the same close, had a famous
attempt at it, too. His toes hit the edge of the midden and
he went PLOOOONK; the toes were hanging on and then
he lost his grip and his chin hit the edge. He was in a semi-
conscious state when we got down to him, eating tea
leaves in the midden. He didn't know what time of day it
was at all.

When, years later, I moved into Hyndland Road in the
West End of Glasgow, I told my wife we had a Lucky
Midden. It was just a rented house that we'd moved to
from Maryhill Road, but it was a really nice area and I was
actually living in a house whose midden I had raided when
I was a wee boy.

The Lucky Middens were where all the posh people lived
and they would throw out really nice things sometimes. I
got a great primus stove once, a real beauty, made of chrome,
which I used for many years when I was cycling around.
And I found a beautiful stainless steel Spitfire – which my
father threw out.

I almost got a guy the jail once, too. I think he was a docker
whose house had been raided or else he was hiding stuff . . .

anyway, he had these big two-pound tins of jam in his midden. My aunt threw them out into our midden, wouldn't let me keep them and wouldn't open them, and some other kids found them and their parents took them to the police. Red plum jam, I'll never forget it. And it was stamped on the top; it had come from Canada and must have been military supplies or something. The police came round to our house and asked me where I got them and I told them the midden. And it would have been really easy to go up the stair and ask everybody 'What dae ye dae for a livin'?' And the docker would be away with the prize.

There were all sorts of things you could find in middens. And I would always get thrashed when I got home, my shoes would be all grey with ash and it would be:

'Ye've been in the midden!'
'No – I havenae!'
'Liar!'
THUMP!

I used to wonder how my parents had this amazing psychic ability to tell where I had been playing. And of course all the time I must have smelt exactly like a bloody midden!

Another one was Setting Fire to the Middens. You would put a light to about twelve of them in one back court and then look at it. It was magic. And you could go off and watch it from a distance, all glowing . . . Aye, we made our own entertainment then.

Tying two doors together was another great favourite. You would get two doors opposite each other on a tenement landing, tie the both of them with a piece of rope, ring the bells, stand back and watch. You would do it not quite terribly tight, so that they could open it just a little and be pulling against each other. I loved that. And I remember watching two guys pulling against each other, the two doors slamming, then a knife coming out round the door trying to cut the rope. The guy's shouting and swearing and there's this wee knife working away. Hysterical it was.

The girls didn't take much part in it all. They would do girlie things, like singing a lot. They would play ball against the wall and sing these lovely songs while they were doing it:

A shepherdess was walking
Ding dong, ding dong,
Come along,
Ding dong.

All those wee daft songs. And in the summer evenings they would all join hands and sing and chant 'Be-Baw Babbity'. But the boys were very much boys and the girls were – well, they just got on with it. Occasionally we would play with them; some of the guys were very good at skipping and no one ever called you a pansy for doing it; they'd call you a pansy if you were *bad* at it.

By the time we were leaving primary school, the boy-girl thing had started to heat up a bit – 'D'ye want to come to the swing-park?' – the notes in school, the wee sniggers. Lovely, halcyon days.

Another of my fondest memories was of the great game of Who Can Pee the Highest which I would play with my pal Gerald McGee, as well. It required great skill . . . pissssshhhhhhhhh . . . then my father caught us doing it one day and walloped me. End of story.

My real hero at the time was this guy Bennet who had a stall in the Barrowlands, selling just about everything. He used to give stuff away free all the time, biros and things like that, to the people hanging round the stall. And one day he actually gave me his own toasted corned beef sandwich. I was so proud.

Graffiti was something we never really got into. The spray guns are a comparatively new thing and anyway I always hated them. But my name is still on the tenement where I used to live – in *tar*. I did it when I was a wee boy. The tar was melting in the street and I picked it up with a stick and wrote my name . . . and Kay Whitelaw's name is there as well. But that wasn't what you would call graffiti, I don't think.

We never used to have pets in the house when I was wee – nothing compared to the menagerie we have at the moment – although we had the occasional cat who would come in, stay for a while and then go away. And they were made very welcome. There was a legendary dog in the family somewhere, but that was dead before I was born.

Since I got married, I've always had a dog. I originally got one because we used to live on the ground floor of a tenement and there used to be these mysterious knocking noises in the middle of the night. And I really felt bad about going away on all these one-nighters while my wife was sitting alone in the house. So I bought a labrador and gradually grew to be quite a doggie sort of person and came round to thinking that without a dog, life wouldn't be quite the same. So I got another labrador . . .

But I don't like these big wild dogs at all. It's always guys with scrapyards that seem to have them, these big alsations – 'This dug could *kill* ye' – kind of number. And I'm not into the poodle side of dog either. I remember once going shopping for a Christmas present for Iris when I was in London and seeing this woman with a poodle in Oxford Street – and the poodle had a *wrist watch* on!

The thing that has always confused me about dogs is that it's always the *people* who win the prizes at the Dog Shows, not the dogs. They should invent a doggie beverage and get all the winners blotto. Or the best dog should get a night with the best bitch.

I like that story about the woman with the two dachshunds, one a dog, one a bitch. And her friend asks her what she does when the bitch is on heat.

'Oh, I just put her in the upstairs bedroom.'
'Yes, but can't the dog get up the stairs when you're out of the house and . . .'
'Have you ever seen a dachshund trying to get upstairs with a hard on?'

One of the things I like about living in the country is the animals you see out there. I saw two wee bambi kind of deer the other night. Jumped out of the car and beat them over the head with a stick with a nail through it . . . no, that's not true.

My great childhood reading matter was the *Beano* and *Dandy*, of course. My father used to pick them up every Friday. It was magic. Then you graduated to the *Wizard* and the *Rover*, which, when I was a boy, didn't have any pictures. They were incredible comics then – the Incredible

Wilson, Jimmy's Magic Patch. I felt really cheated when the *Rover* and the *Hotspur* and the *Wizard* went over to being all pictures, even though I wasn't reading them any more. I thought that was robbery.

When I was fourteen I was delivering the milk, living in Drumchapel and working in Bearsden. You started at quarter-to-four in the morning and finished just in time to get to school. I thoroughly enjoyed it. Thirty bob a week you got, which was really quite good. And when I was delivering milk in Drumchapel, I would get a wee tip every week, when I went to collect the money . . . and big tips in Bearsden at Christmas.

I had to stop it eventually, though. We were doing a bit of pranking, throwing snowballs at each other and I was carrying my bottles, running away from this snowball attack. And I tripped – tried to jump over a fence and didn't quite make it. My toes got caught on the top of the fences and – WHUMP – I fell on top of the milk bottles and burst the tendon in my index finger. Had to go to hospital and get a tendon transplant from my foot to my hand. That was the end of my career in milk.

For a while I sold papers, too, running along, shouting. We did the *Evening News*, the *Evening Times* and the *Citizen* and we used to go, 'TIMES NEWS AND CITI-ZEN'. When the *Evening News* folded I couldn't get my chant right for a long time, so I added 'Final' and went, 'TIMES AND CITIZEN FIN-AL'. That balanced up.

I didn't have a round of my own at first, that was in Drumchapel; but then I got to deliver them to the houses. There was more money in that, because you got a tip when you collected the money every Friday. And I've yet to see someone tipping a boy selling papers in the street. The cream of the paper-sellers, though, were always the ones who had the Sunday stalls near the churches. They made a packet.

It was never mentioned at school what they wanted you to do when you left. But they would have you believe that engineering was one of the highest pinnacles you could aspire to – next to teaching! Engineering is a superb thing to do, but I don't like the way that they set that as the highest site for you to aim for. They were more or less saying – 'Look, you're a dumpling and you'd better believe it.' I don't like that.

Another thing I continually heard teachers saying was 'What do you want to be when you leave – a *dustman*?' What the hell's wrong with being a dustman? My sister Flo, who's a teacher, has had the experience of a wee boy in tears because his father was a dustman. All because this half-wit of a teacher is going round telling them that a dustman is some kind of a balloon.

The police came round to St Gerard's, just before we left, to tell us all how cosy it was being a policeman. The guy wasn't exactly laughed off – just laughed off in complete silence. They were regarded as the common enemy. It was Them and Us, very much so.

But the Partick police when I was a boy were terrific. They were magic big guys. Talk about 'finger on the pulse' – they knew exactly what was going on. It was the end of the kick-in-the-arse era, just before the beginning of 'If I catch you I'm goin' tae tell yer faither.' There was none of the 'You're goin' tae jail' number or anything like that. It was the old boot in the backside and many's the time I got a

47

smack on the lug from a policeman. Not that it changed my ways, but I'm really thankful that he didn't run upstairs like a big lassie and tell my father.

I suppose I was always the funny one in the class at school and always looking for a bit of attention from people. And I still love the jokes about that sort of age . . .

Like there was a wee boy in Glasgow, ten years old and he's out alone at night when he runs into this policeman.

'What are ye doin' out at this hour, eh?'
'I'm lookin' for a prostitute.'
'What's a wee boy like you lookin' for a prostitute for, for heaven's sake?'
'I want tae catch VD off her so that I can gi'e it tae our au pair and then she can gi'e it tae ma faither and he can gi'e it tae ma mother and she can gi'e it tae the gardener because HE KILLED MA TORTOISE!'

MY PLUKEY YOUTH Twisting for Scotland, Pyjamas in Jail & a Half-Brick Neatly Aimed

There was this legendary careers master at school, but I didn't ever see him. In fact, I don't think I ever met anyone who did see him. So when the time came for me to leave, I just left. Didn't speak to anyone, didn't even say Cheerio. It was just that I Was Leaving and That Was It.

So I went to the Youth Employment Office, who offered me a job in John Collier's and in a butchers. I didn't want to be a butcher. So the guy says:

'Well, what do you want to be then?'
'I don't know really. I think I'd like tae be an engineer.'

But they had no vacancies for engineers and there was *no way* that I was going to work for John Collier's . . . so I saw an advertisement for a bookshop messenger in the papers.

I went right down and got the job, delivering books for a few months for about thirty bob a week. I loved it, going about on my bike. Then I got sacked. And to this day I swear I didn't steal the books. It was near Christmas and there was a big rip-off in the despatch department and the buck stopped at the message boy – it can't go any further. So I got the heave-ho.

Then I got a job as delivery boy for Bilsland's Bread, which I loved. Going along with the van driver and carrying loaves. And then it was from there to the Clyde and my apprenticeship.

I get a bit fed up being asked about the shipyards and what it was like as a welder and all that. Because I've been out of

49

the yards for as long as I was in them. And as far as I'm concerned, I don't want to be just the comic-who-used-to-be-a-welder-in-the-Clyde-shipyards.

But there are certain characters in the yards that I always get asked about now: you know, the Great Voltaine. The guy who would do this amazing performance in the dinner-break, dressed in a cape.

'Think of a number.'
'Thirteen.'
'Correct!'

And the guy who was a wee bit simple and we used to let him play in the football matches we had at dinner-time and he would just run around waving his arms everywhere. And the welders made him this lovely Player of the Year trophy and carried him round the yards . . .
'HULLOOOOO . . . Player of the Year . . . '

Lucas and Dalgleish now, I'm always being asked about them. They were two great guys in the yards, who were so funny I would hurry to my work just to hear their patter. They would be working on a boat and suddenly you'd see them at the far end of it with their arms round each other, dancing, on this great liner . . . 'We'll meet again, don't know where, don't know when . . . '

I loved it all. The guy in the blacksmith's shop with the wee piece of wire round his head so that he could keep a cigarette in it and smoke while he was working . . .

But, at first, my parents weren't terribly keen about going into the yards. But it had always had a fascination for me. If you live on the Clyde, there's this thing about working

in the shipyards, which I suppose you get in Yorkshire and
Durham, with working in the mines, and in Peterhead and
Fraserburgh, working on the fishing boats.

I still go down to the yards to have a drink in the pubs there,
or just to drive past. I used to have this sticker from the
film *O Lucky Man*, which I had on my guitar case; and I
used to look at the guys going in for the night shift and
think, Aye, right enough, because I do feel really lucky to
be doing what I'm doing now.

So I started work as an apprentice at Stephens yard. Five
years it was. And up on the North Sea oil thing, they're
making welders foremen with only two weeks' training!

The work and the people there were great. It was a whole
wee world inside the yards, you could get anything you
wanted there.

The heavy number was something I never really got
involved in. Sure, I was in a few fights at the dancing, a
few smackaboos. But that was OK. No slashing or stabbing,
just getting right in there with the boot. That was as heavy
as it got. The really heavy guys and me never really had
that much in common, even at school. And when I left, my
friends were mostly from the shipyards and the guys who
were into the heavies and into battering people were
normally unemployed or stuff like that.

There were some legendary heavies around, though. The
Mad Spaniard was one. What a name, eh? I was going with
a wee girl from the Maryhill Road and he was killed right
outside her house.

But with moving house – I left Partick for Drumchapel when I was fourteen – I had to start to make a whole lot of new friends, which was quite strange; at that age you should have forged most of your friendships. But I had to break them off and start again. So my friends were boys I knew from school in Govan, who lived at the Drum. So I never really got involved in the local gang thing, the wee fly men doing things to one another.

The fights at the dance hall were usually because you lived in a certain area, or were a Catholic or a Protestant, depending on who they were looking for at the time. It was never for something like taking someone else's woman or anything like that, it never got to the women at all. It was always just guys desperately wanting to beat someone up. It was all:

'D'ye think that style will ever come back, eh?' as they look at your suit.

'Who ye talkin' tae, pal?'

'You – what d'ye want tae dae aboot it?'

And then you'd see them moving in and you'd think, Oh, fuck, what have I done. Or they would go:

'Did ye get the haircut that was in the windae, eh, pal?'

Just needle-needle to get you to do something and then they'd beat the seven colours of shit out of you.

One thing that struck me as being particularly evil – when I was still in Partick this was, at the time of the Teds – was that the wee neds used to sew fish-hooks behind their lapels for when someone was going to grab them by their jacket to nut them. Can you imagine being impaled on those things?

The Hell's Angels in Glasgow were really funny. They were very scruffy and called themselves the Blue Angels, but they were really just a poor replica of the real thing.

They used to go down to Olympia every year for the motorbike show to beat up the Hell's Angels – 'stiffen a few Londoners, eh?' But at one point they had no bikes, but just this one big van. And they would come to the pub and all troop out of the van wearing all the leather jackets and the Nazi helmets and the boots and everything – out of this dormobile! They had about three bikes between them, eventually, one of them a lovely three-wheeler with a Mini engine.

The British Hell's Angels are a joke. The American ones are the real thing. A friend of mine met one of them, Sonny Barger, when he was playing a gig in San Quentin jail and all the prisoners were coming up to him and saying 'What drugs do you want? Cocaine? Acid?' But I'm no great lover of these people and I don't like the way that in America they've been assimilated into the hippie way of culture.

I was a biker as well. I used to have a side car and go to gigs in it. But in my younger days I had a BSA Roadrocket, though in actual fact it was a Spitfire with an American engine and twin carbs, 650 cc . . . I had all the leathers . . . a few smashes, too. Took off on a hump once, coming round a corner at 85 m.p.h. and the bike dug in and jumped. Thirty-six stitches in my arm for my trouble. That was the beginning of the end.

At first, though, I had a wee tiny bike. I was a real chancer and I was in this gang called The Men. What a name, eh?

They all had big bikes and I had this wee one. But we weren't really a violent kind of gang at all, we weren't into beating people up or any of the sub-culture. We just liked bikes. We would just get on our bikes, ride somewhere, have a cup of tea and come back. We had a lot of wild parties, but then again everyone has wild parties, not just guys with motorbikes.

Then the *Sunday Mail* got hold of us. It was at the time when *The Wild One*, the Marlon Brando film about motorbikes, was making a lot of news; it had been banned, I think, but anyway it was on at the Grand Central in Glasgow and everyone had seen it. So they set up this photo of us standing beside a sign on the road which read: JESUS DIED FOR OUR SINS. We were in the leathers, the whole number. And now I drive past it on the way from Glasgow to Drymen. It must have been twelve years ago, but wee Billy remembers the photo, too. They were great days, great laughs.

My criminal record started when I was playing football in a private ground and I was fined half a crown at the Marine Police Court in Partick: 'That'll be a lesson to you, you vandal.' Aye, so that was two and six.

After that, I got done for syphoning petrol. It was really a shame. I'd run out of petrol for my bike and was going round these garages and saying: 'Look, you can have my licence if you give me a gallon of petrol. I'll go home, get the money, bring it back and get my licence back.' NO. They wouldn't even let me park my bike in the garage for the night. And there was no way I could push it all the way back to Drumchapel. So I went and got myself a wee hose and a can. And got caught. Fined £15.

Then I assaulted a guy in Bearsden. It was my only night in jail, in a police station in Milngavie. It was very funny because the police came to my house to get me and I was already in my pyjamas. So I looked out of the window when I heard all the noise, put my jeans on over the tops of the pyjamas and got ready to go away with them.

So I got into the cell and took off my shirt and my jeans and there I had my pyjamas on underneath. I was lying on the bed, getting ready to go to sleep and one of the policemen came and looked in through the wee spy-hole in the door . . .

'Well, I've seen them come and I've seen them go . . . but never in pyjamas.'

Fined £15.

How it happened was that I was going with this girl and this guy had landed her one, smacked her about the mouth a bit. So I was kind of forced into it. I was frightened but I was in this cornered situation. So I belted him and he hit me and I belted him again. And there was another guy with me. We were given a year's suspended sentence and fined. But the other guy went and stole a motorbike so he got sent to a Young Offenders' Institution and I had been clean so I got admonished. I was just eighteen.

The guy I beat up was a real animal, but his father was quite a wealthy bloke. Nobody deserved a smack in the mouth as much as he did, ever. If I ever see him again, I'd be delighted to do the same, absolutely delighted. And I'm not a very violent person. I just detested the guy.

That was it. That was the end of my involvement with Crime and Punishment.

But I have been up on quite a few breach of the peaces since. For shouting and bawling: £2 fines and a lecture – 'How very, very dare you!' and 'Aren't you ashamed of yourself?' And of course you agree with everything the guy says.

The assault I dearly wish I hadn't done because that sort of thing sticks about on your record. It would have been so easy to walk away. They would have called me a coward, but who cares? But when you're younger, your head's full of Hollywood. It's all 'They can put me in jail for loving you, but they'll never stop my face from breaking out.'

Another time I was in court was as a character witness – for a thug. The guy had been assaulted by the police and I genuinely liked him and thought he was a smashing bloke, so I went along and spoke for him and he just got fined, didn't go to jail.

As far as I could see, it was the police that had assaulted him, although he was up for assaulting the police. It was him that had the stitches, so what were they complaining about? They won, didn't they?

He had long hair, when it was dreadfully unfashionable to do so, and an earring. And he was attacked on a bus by this woman: 'You filthy wretch, away and try a bath' kind of thing. He just sat there and let her get through with it and she went on and on. So eventually he swore at her, told her to fuck off. Then her husband comes up with the 'Don't you speak to my wife like that' number. So – he belted him. THUMP. And coming off the bus the husband leapt on his back, so he belted him again. The police came round, because by this time it was looking as if Ronnie was doing an all-out attack on an innocent, short-haired member of society. So the police got into Ronnie and he, of course, retaliated. They won; they had the big sticks.

But I generally try and avoid that sort of thing like the plague. Even when there's a fight in a pub, even if it's away over the other side of the bar, I'm off right away. Offski.

People insult me in bars quite a lot, but they don't usually try to pick fights. You get the characters who say:

'Hey, I saw you last night on television.'
'Yeah?'
'You were rubbish!'

Right in front of everyone. You feel such a dog. It would be the easiest thing in the world to run up and give them a smack in the mouth, it would be delightful. But I think the wise thing is just to get up and walk away.

But the whole courts thing should be looked into. The working-class boy from Partick gets completely different treatment for doing the same thing as the middle-class boy from Bearsden.

We would go to Rothesay for September or Easter weekends and have a right laugh. HULLLOOOOO! Shouting and bawling and throwing toilet rolls. Several of us would get arrested and go to court, get fined and it was Vandalism. But meanwhile, the middle-class kids from Bearsden would go to Millport and do exactly the same thing. But that was High Spirits.

It's the same thing with rugby and football. The rugby teams can go about smashing up hotels and nothing happens to them; they're even applauded for it. A football player does it and he's banned for life from playing for his country – not fair, *not on*. The SFA can do more to see that the Scottish team gets beaten than any other team could. I'm not saying that players should be untouched, but at least they should get the same treatment as they give the rugby players.

I've played in various prisons and I've played a remand home for boys that were Going To The Bad. But I didn't feel good playing in there at all. I don't feel bad playing in a jail, because the guys in there are adult enough to know why they're in there, they know what the odds are. They don't feel sorry for themselves, so why should I? I love performing in jail; it's just like performing at a theatre only the situation is reversed: at the end of the show you rush off and the audience stays behind.

Barlinnie – even sounds like a jail, doesn't it? – I enjoy playing in. And I'm always surprised by the requests I get from the guys inside. It's always for very complex things that I can't do at all, Leonard Cohen and stuff like that. The blokes in there are great, a great audience to play to, very appreciative. And I keep meeting people who saw me play when they were in jail. I really have to hold myself back from pontificating at them:

'I hope you're on the straight and narrow now, eh?'

How dare I! And it really infuriates me when I read stuff in the papers about the prisoners having such a great life and watching colour telly all the time while the rest of us have to get up and do a day's work. That's all complete rubbish.

Remember Peter Manuel? Every time I pass Glasgow High Court, to this day, I think of him. He had that much of an effect on everyone in Scotland, he must have been one of our most famous murderers of all time. There was that amazing photo of him: the eyes, the cravat, the blazer. Astonishing character.

And a guy I really admired was Johnny Ramensky, the safe-blower who was let out of jail in the war so that he could work behind enemy lines. But by the same token I was desperately disappointed in him when he got older and kept getting caught all the time. There was a good book there, which I wish someone could have done and given him a few quid so that he could relax.

There was a great song about him, which Roddy Macmillan wrote and Hamish Imlach and Josh Macrae used to sing:

Open up your prison gates
And let Ramensky go.

I've kept out of trouble pretty well myself. There was one time in Glasgow when Iris and I were in a fish shop and this wee ned comes in, goes right up to the counter, in front of the rest of us queueing there and orders his supper. Iris goes, 'Hey, there's a queue —' Just ignores her completely and as he goes out he kicks the dog. So I ran out into the street after him to give him the message. But by this time he was too far away for me to catch up with him. And there was this building-site right beside the fish shop. So I picked up a half-brick and threw it at him. Caught him perfectly on the back of the head. Smackeroo.

Of course there were all sorts of fiddles at the yards, that was expected. One time some guys even stole a grand piano from off a boat. It was in the captain's cabin or the lounge or somewhere and they got all the gear and winched it out and drove it off. Stopped at the gate of the yard and they just said: 'Off for repairs.' – 'Very good.' Off they went.

One of the wee numbers we used to do was making coins out of metal that would fit into cigarette machines. They had to be done to the right weight and everything, but you didn't need the sort of ridges bit on the outside of a two bob bit, because a lot of the machines won't take them and if a real coin is a bit worn, the machine rejects it. If you're really smart you can make a mould of a coin and freeze water in it and if you're quick enough in putting it into the cigarette machine, you'll get the fags and all they find the next day is this little puddle. 'Hey, what's a' this water?'

To get back to the dancing, which would be at the Barrowland Locarno . . . the music was all big bands, playing the hits of the day: Billy McGregor's Band and George MacCallum's Metronomes. This was just before the Twist and at the time the great hit was 'Please Help Me, I'm Falling' by Hank Locklin. I toured with him later on and told him how much his music had affected me and I think I bored the arse off him.

We used to dance the Moony. The women would put their hands round the men's necks and you put both your hands on her bum and you dance cheek to cheek; a very sensible form of dancing it was. And I remember sniggering when my aunt referred to it as 'moondancing'.

'Ye're away daein' that moondancin', are ye?'

I think the *News of the World* had exposed it: 'THEY HOLD EACH OTHER'S BUMS!'

Now the Glide was quite intricate. You really needed to
be able to dance to get up for the Glide. It wasn't like
today when you can just get up and chance your arm. And
we used to do the whole number: a few bevvys first, of
course, and perhaps a half-bottle of wine, electric soup, in
the toilet. Fiesta we used to drink – three and six a half-
bottle. Then it was up to the jigeroo, up to the balcony
and have a look down, to see the women. Then you'd spot
one and be down right away, split up the two women
dancing and glide off.

It was like a cattle market. The women all stood along the
edge of the wall and the guys all stood on the edge of the
dance floor. There was a sort of no-man's-land in between.
There used to be a lot of refusing going on, too, when guys
would go up to ask for a dance. And there was this legend
that, if a woman refused to dance, you could go up to the
management and have her flung out. But who would do
that? Who would own up to it? And yet everyone knew
someone who knew someone who had been flung out,
although I never saw it myself. Aye, it was a long road
back if you were refused.

That was all well before the Women's Lib thing . . . though
when I was in Denmark, the women there were very
liberated already. They would come up and tweak your
bum as you were going past and they would chat you up,
too. I liked that. It was so strange and different . . .

So the procedure was one dance, then offski. And if she
stayed on for a second with you, you went 'Oh-ho-ho-
hooooo' . . . you might get it. If she stayed on for a third
one – *guaranteed*. Then it was:

'Would you like something to drink? Coke? Coffee, eh?
Would you like a hamburger? No? Sure? Glass of milk?'

That's when I discovered cold milk. You know those
machines; I couldn't believe it was so *tasty*. Then you
would have another wee dance ...

'Er ... where do you live?'
'So-and-so.'
'Very good.'

If it was near, you got a taxi; if it was far away, you got a
bus. So off you would go with her and try and do something
in a back close.

Another thing I discovered was that Laundromats are
great places for pulling women. You would go in and look
all helpless:

'Er ... does this ... go in that bit?'
'No, no – in there.'
'And I put the powder in ...'
'No – look, I'll show you.'

The clothes situation was all suits. The tie-and-hankie
had just made a breakthrough so you had that with the
three-button suit with the vents in the jacket. Tapered
trousers. Small turn-ups. Striped material was all the
rage, preferably blue, vertical stripes.

My pride and joy was a Crombie jacket, made out of that
very heavy overcoat material. Oh, I loved it dearly. Then
a weird style came in – drape trousers, twenty at the knee
and fourteen or fifteen inches at the bottom. And of course
the winkle-pickers! But when I first went dancing, it was

big flat shoes called the Palermo, absolutely plain and very wide, with a broad flat heel. White shoes for men caused a sensation. I had a pair of white moccasins which I wore with a lilac tie and a paper collar, which you got in a packet of six from Woolworths. You needed the six, because you got through about five trying them on.

The women would wear the big dirndl skirts with millions of underskirts. Then it became a brown Glen check, which was all the rage: jacket, skirt, white shoes. The real neat military-looking affair.

And, oh, the scenes in the gents. Jostling for the mirror, all the combs flashing about everywhere, examining the plukes, going through the Brylcreem.

Around eighteen or nineteen, I went to classes to learn how to jive. Jive had come and gone by then but I still wanted to do it.

And while I was there, the Twist came in and one of the guys in the class was twisting in the 'off-beat' section of 'Come Dancing' on the telly. Because I was in the jiving class, I was around as well and was made reserve for the team. Then a guy got sick and so I went on, did it on the telly – I Twisted for Scotland! We won our section, too.

There were some great parties, too. One of the best this friend of mine had. It was a few years on from all this and he was getting married the following day; so it was his stag do.

The party was going fine, lots of bevvy and everyone was singing. Someone said: 'Would anybody like chips?' With all the drinking, we'd got a bit hungry. So two guys were delegated to go down town and get all these fish suppers, pies, black puddings.

A little later they all come back and they've got this extra guy they've met somewhere with them. He's a spastic sort of fellow, with bad legs and crutches.

'We thought we'd invite him along, too. He's a nice sort of guy.'

'Aye, sure, sure, very good. Come in.'

Anyway, we all get back to the drinking. The fish suppers are in the gas oven to heat up, because they've got cold what with the journey back and them picking up this spastic. The party's well in progress and this guy with the crutches turns out to be a sort of homosexual, going around falling on top of everybody. Like he's kidding on that he's tripping and stumbling and his hand just always happens to land on someone's private parts. There's a couple of guys having a piss in the toilet together:

'That wee spastic guy gave me an awful bump there, y'know.'

'Oh? He did that tae me as well ...'

So he was thrown out and while he was being ejected from the premises, there was a smell of burning. So everyone dives into the kitchen. It was the fish suppers. They'd left the paper on them, they were all still wrapped up and the paper was on fire.

So in order to douse the flames, they threw them into this big pot of soup on the stove. SPLOOOT! They got as many of the black bits of burnt paper out as they could and served up the soup with the fish suppers floating in it.

We're well drunk by this time and all going like the clappers. Now the guy's parents are in the room, too. And at this point the boy's mother is raving a bit – her wee boy's getting married in the morning . . .

'Well, he can have all the furniture he likes. But I am keeping that coffee table that he made when he was at school.'

The words were about two seconds out of her mouth when my pal Mick Broderick sits on it. The four legs went in four different directions. There was this awful CRUNCHHHHH sound. The mother nearly fainted, it was all 'OHMYGOD'.

Eventually someone pacifies her a bit and someone else notices a picture on the wall of a kiltie with the bagpipes, all military with the kilt and the bonnet with the feather in it.

'Who's *that*?'
'It's me,' says the father of the house.
'Och, *away*!'
'Aye, so it is!'
'Where's yer pipes?'
'Och, they're in the cupboard somewhere . . .'

Away to the cupboard, gets the pipes out, sticks them all together and off he goes: 'Tee-tuddle-a-tuddle-a-tuddle-a-tee, tuddle-a-tuddle-a-dee' . . . Marching round the house with the pipes and everyone's half-drunk and shouting at him to give it laldie and screaming 'HULLLOOOO'. So he did a kind of fancy bagpipe half-turn at the end of the room and the end of his bagpipes knocks the wedding picture off the wall and it smashes on the floor. The glass is being all crunched in by the marchers following the pipes. The wife nearly faints again: 'OHMYGOD!'

So she goes to belt her husband but bumps into someone else and there's a whole series of bumps, like dominoes, and at the end of it all was Mick Broderick, who was leaning with his elbow on the mantelpiece. And his elbow goes right along the mantelpiece, knocking off all these wee crinoline ladies as it goes – SMASH CRASH on the floor.

At that, the whole place goes berserk. People start to fight, it's help-murder-polis. And Mick Broderick, drunk, has gone to the window and he walks slap into this bicycle that's hanging there on a pulley outside; it was quite a common thing to do in tenement buildings – you'd hang the bike outside and have more room in the hall. He's walked right into the pedal and the chain and hurt his face. Anyway, we're all thrown out. End of picture.

My own stag night was in a pub and everyone got completely drunk. I woke up in some shop doorway and almost got lifted by the police. Still, that's what everyone does. I got married in a registry office; I think it would have been pretty hypocritical to get married in a church, although I know lots of guys who thought the same as me and went ahead with it.

I was mainly into cycling when I was in my teens. I was quite healthy, didn't smoke at all. Cycled around all over Scotland and loved it. I wore the whole number; the wee hat, the chamois seat on the trousers, the diced hose, the wee Reg Harris Fallowfield shoes, Chanelli handle-bars.

It took up most of my money at the time. I was only getting £2.6.5d a week and my father would give me another quid. The bike was costing about fourteen bob a week, because I was paying it up; it wasn't a regular bike – I had a shop build it for me.

Then around that time, when I was eighteen or nineteen, I started smoking; it wasn't until then. My shipyard had a Boys' Club for the apprentices and we used to go up to Cambusbarron to a place which had been an army camp during the war. And that's where my pal, Joe West, started me off on smoking. Joe was quite a pal. We started school on the same day, passed our qualifying on the same day, left school on the same day, started our apprenticeship on the same day at Stephens, and finished our apprenticeship on the same day. Kind of weird, right through from the age of five till I was twenty-one, we were doing everything the same.

So, with my cycling, I was getting around all over Scotland and eventually wanted to see a bit more. So I went off on this hitching holiday. I had seven quid in my pocket, a sleeping-bag and a copy of *Catch-22*. That was all my worldly goods.

Fortunately, these chip-shops in Belgium get pre-made chips delivered to them, all cut and washed, wrapped in big polythene bags, early in the morning. But the shop doesn't open till dinner-time so I would be along first thing in the morning . . . I virtually lived on chips.

67

And while I was hitching between France and Belgium,
I would come across these little shrines; they must have
been for Flemish saints or something like that. They would
be in the corners of fields, where people would leave apples
and oranges and wee pieces of bread. So I got tore into
that lot right away. Maybe that's what they were for, who
knows?

I thoroughly enjoyed myself and enjoyed the fact that I was
skint. It made you feel really free. I had my cousin with me
and a friend called Alan Cherry, but they got stuck in
Dunkirk, getting drunk for about six weeks on their Big
Continental Tour. But I couldn't take that at all – Dunkirk
is a desperately boring place – so I went off to Belgium and
just hung around.

It was a great holiday really. I didn't get down to Spain
although I went there a few years later with Iris and the
kids and all the beaches smelled like sewers. Apparently, in
the old days, the Spaniards used to leave the best land they
had to their eldest sons and the youngest ones, the ones the
fathers didn't like, would be given the beach, which was
worth nothing. So now the guys with all the beaches and the
money are the real bastards.

I couldn't get over in Spain how the whole place had been
taken over by Germans – the whole place stank of grilled
Germans. They would get up early in the morning to book
their deck-chair on the beach, put a newspaper on it or
something, and then go back to bed and come down and
claim it later. Quite amazing.

But then I was just staying in Youth Hostels and sleeping
out. The hostels were very boring, because you had to be in
by ten o'clock, which is the time when everything is

beginning to rumble on the Continent. And you have to go off to beddy-byes with your book on butterflies. And some of the people who run the hostels are these fascist types, very cold eyes, sort of jailer types.

We used to make these noises at night with our cheeks. You pull them and go: 'choooogie-chooogie, chooogie-chooogie'. All the lights would go on. Everybody's looking.

'Who's *doing* that?'

But my favourite ploy was one which, like all good practical jokes, you never saw the result of, because the guy would be somewhere else when it happened: we used to find somebody sleeping with his socks on, take one off and put it on top of the other without him waking up. So he would get up in the morning – 'Where's my bloody sock?' – have to put his boots on with one foot bare. And then he would get home and find out and think, THOSE BASTARDS!

Another thing we used to do was put a matchbox inside someone's underpants when they were asleep. They would wake up and think Jesus Christ, what's going on here, for God's sake. They'd be tossing and turning about in their bed.

And you know the Youth Hostel situation where you've got pigeon holes where you put your food? Everyone would store their food in this rack on the wall and you each have your own little space. But there's no shutter on it so you can see everyone's food. Therefore you can steal everyone's food. So John, my cousin, and I would get a pin, steal an egg, puncture it at both ends, blow the egg

69

into the frying pan and then put a wee note inside the egg and put it back. The guy's coming up to get his egg and cook it for breakfast: smash, he cracks it open – what's this? There's a letter in it:

'I'm sorry, but I was awful hungry.'

Slicing the Banana While It's Still In Its Skin was another good one we used to do. You do it with a needle and go down the seams of the banana so that you can't notice anything from the outside, and just slice it neatly. So the guy gets his banana, peels it and sees that it all falls in slices . . .

'Hey, did you see that?'
'No,' you say, 'what was it?'
'I just peeled the banana and it was all sliced up inside!'
'Och, away.'
He feels dreadful.
'Honest! It really was sliced!'
'Oh, sure, sure. Very good . . .' Then he's beginning to doubt it himself.

But one of the classic ones was practised in Partick. People would put dogshit on the padlocks of doors. So when the policemen came round to check the locks at night, in the dark, they'd pull at the padlock – it was called 'milking the padlock' – give it a wee pull to see if it was all right. And then they'd realize:

'Oh, NAWWWWWWW......'

DRINK Shuggie Gilchrist's Drinking Coat,
the Monday Club & Only Poofs Can't Tap-Dance

The Portland Arms in Troon was where I had my first
drink. I was a cyclist at the time and mixing with that sort
of bloke, the campers, the other cyclists who certainly didn't
drink very much, except for the older guys. So I didn't
bother with the drink at all. It wasn't what I looked on as a
good time. I knew that I would drink in later years and I
looked forward to being in pubs and being adult. But I
didn't go through the Partick pre-pub age drinking thing,
the wine-drinking, the vino collapso number – though a lot
of my friends did. So I didn't get involved at all until I was
eighteen or nineteen.

The pubs were always for men only, very much so, though
there were always lounges around the place where guys
went with their wives and girlfriends – the Family
Department it was called.

But when I first started drinking, it was always cider I
would get tore into – Scrumpy – before I went dancing.
And wine sometimes in the Barrowlands Bar: Lanliq was
the new thing and my wife was very keen on it – Lang's
Liqueur it was. So I started drinking that and I thought
it was smashing, but it gave you a terrible sore head in the
morning, all that sugar.

It was funny the way all the different guys progressed with
their drinking. Some went right on to whisky. Some would
imitate the older guys and have the half-pint and the
whisky. Then someone would want a large one – 'Eh, large
whisky, pal' – HULL-OO – and after that it was always a
large one for him.

Some guys really went in for the drinkipoos. Twelve was the legendary number of pints. Joe West, my pal, held the record for the number of pints of scrumpy drunk: six it was. We didn't do much more than that because we would be drinking before we went dancing and if you went over the top, you couldn't dance. And you wouldn't be able to pull any lumber.

Shug Gilchrist had a special drinking coat that he kept in the Saracen's Head, a big plastic mac which was kept faithfully in the back room for him. And when he came in he would put it on before he started drinking, because he had some lovely, lovely suits. He used to button it right up to the neck, because at the Saracen's Head, they would be passing the drinks over your head and going: 'Pints? Right, here ye are . . .' – SLUUUOOORP – splashing over everyone.

One place I used to drink in was the Scotia Bar. It used to be great when the Drugs Squad came in there; everyone would whistle the theme from *Z-Cars*. Or somebody would suddenly shout out:

'Anyone who can't tap-dance is a poof!'

And there would be all these plainclothes guys with short hair, really straight-looking blokes, trying to tap-dance along with the rest of us so that they wouldn't look conspicuous.

Another of my regular places was the Downhill Bar in Partick. This pal of mine started the Monday Club there – I don't know if it was his idea, but anyway he was the guy who started it. It was for all the guys in Partick who go to these drinking clubs in Partick on a Sunday night and get so blootered that they just feel so rotten the next day, the Monday, that they don't go to their work. So they meet in the Downhill Bar in the morning.

But they've pulled down one of my favourites, the Marland Bar, which is where I used to drink. It was a great place where all the hairies went when there weren't many of them around. I loved it there and learnt a lot about music and playing from the guys there. Then they knocked it down and the hairies all scattered north and south and east and west.

The London pubs I never really liked very much – the English Dream. I don't think that oak and horse-brasses necessarily make a good pub and it saddens me when I see all that rubbish in Scottish pubs, which is happening a bit in the country. I don't like these ultra-modern pubs either, the Formica Arms, with all the wee Spanish souvenirs, the wee galleons and stuff that they've brought back from Ibiza.

I've never been an enormously heavy drinker and I certainly don't want to become like some of the guys that you meet in the music business, particularly the folk side, who spend all their time on the bottle and you have to peel back the layers of skin to see their eyes.

The capacity of some people amazes me. I drank once with the fishermen at Fleetwood. Amazing blokes, there was no question of you being able to pay for a round. They would come off their boats, drink till they ran out of money and then go back to sea. The place they would drink at was a hotel and they would all buy carry-outs from it when it closed at two-thirty. Then they would sit outside drinking until it opened again three hours later. And the manager of the place would be leaning out of the window chatting to them until he could open again, and back they would all troop. I couldn't keep up at all.

New Year was never a big number in our family. Christmas was the thing, Christmas was nice. It was never ever a party thing, never even a Christmas dinner, it was just a happy time, a happy atmosphere. We very rarely had parties in our family for anything, and I don't even recall having a birthday party ever. We just weren't a party kind of family.

I got to enjoy New Year as I was older. On the night itself I celebrate now, whereas when I was younger it would be the three-day drinkerama. But I can't take those three-day binges any more. I did until up to a couple of years ago. Maybe it's because I'm in my thirties or something, but I don't seem to be able to sustain it any more. I just can't last out on that constant drinking without feeling pretty tragic.

First-footing I've done with a plaster on my leg. I had broken my ankle, fallen off a boat in the Clyde. In fact, it was my first ever write-up in the papers, the *Daily Express* it was . . . and I had one of those plasters on my leg, with one of those wooden rockers on my foot. Eventually that went agley or fell off or something. And I remember as the night wore on it started snowing and the plaster got soaking wet and gradually wider and wider – I was like a platypus – and I had this huge foot. So I had to rip my trousers to get them off.

I nearly choked to death that night, too. I went to be sick over one of these chestnut fences, the wire and the strips of wood. I was like in the stocks. I just collapsed with my neck over it and my arms over it, hanging between the strips of wood. I couldn't breathe. A taxi-driver revived me and I

would probably have died, hanging from this thing . . .
what a mess I was.

There used always to be these guys around at New Year
that would become unconscious early on and they would
just be carted around from house to house and dumped in
the corner of a room until it was time to move on to the
next place. Myself, I have only had one complete total
blotto, right out, blackout, picture's over . . . well, maybe
two. I don't like that forgetting what you've done. It's a
dangerous sign, you feel that you're on the way down and
down. Both times I was drinking Carlsberg – it's a very
powerful drink.

I've never been drunk on stage in my life. Well, that's a
lie . . . I have been drunk lots of times at folk clubs and at
folk festivals, but nobody notices because they're all drunk,
too. One time I was ill and all choked up with the flu,
when I was performing at the Ashfield Club. The guy
wouldn't let me stay off because he said he couldn't find
another act to replace me that would please his punters, so
I went on. And I was staggering around all over the place,
quite sober but feeling awful, and everyone thought I was
bloody drunk.

I did pretend to be drunk once when I was doing this gig at
Rothesay. I was the main act on this boat and I was
staggering up and down the deck, leaning over the side of
the boat, pretending to be sick –
'HUUUUGGGGGHHHHEEEEEE' – heaving and
everything. The promoter was furious.

But if you're performing, drink dulls the reactions. And if
I'm going to be heckled by someone who's drunk and I'm
sober, I'll be ten times faster than him; and I've got the

75

microphone after all so I should never lose against anyone. You have to be that wee bit sharp with them, but by being sharp you encourage them to have another go – if they're not too bright, they get the showbiz bug and want to be part of the show.

Just a while ago a guy came up on the stage – it was frightening – he was drunk, with that red-eyed look about him. He got up and came staggering towards me and I thought, Here we go. And I immediately thought, Don't punch my guitar! I don't worry about being physically hurt or punched or whatever, but if I fall on top of my guitar or fall off the stage and break my leg and can't work, that's something else. But he came up and shook my hand. Oh my God, I was never so happy. He had done it for a bet with his mates.

One of the most tragic things I ever saw in my entire life – Shakespeare couldn't have written it – was when Josh Macrae and I were sitting in the Gem restaurant on the Great Western Road. We were sitting in the window, doing a bit of posing, looking out. Facing us was this street, coming right down to the restaurant.

We saw this wee drunk guy coming down towards us, doing the 'I Am Sober' walk, but veering a bit to starboard because of this bottle of beer he had in his jacket pocket. He stopped at the pavement, and he must have had matches or a hankie or something in the same pocket as the beer because he reached into the pocket and the bottle fell out on to the pavement . . . bong . . . bong . . . bong . . . but it didn't break! And his wee face lit up with this big smile. So he bends down to pick it up and the half-bottle of whisky in his inside pocket falls out – SMASSSSHHH! Josh and I were near greeting.

These licensing laws that we're lumbered with are so crazy. Why will they not let you drink in a pub on a Sunday? All this business about going into hotels to get a drink is such a load of rubbish. If they go into the pubs in England, why can they not in Scotland?

I like the story about the judge coming back from the courts very late one night with vomit all down his jacket, all over his lapels and everything, the diced carrots, the lot. His wife asks him what happened to him:

'This drunken hooligan came up to me in the street and was sick all down my jacket. It was disgusting. But when he comes into the court in front of me, I'm going to fine him £20 and teach him a damn good lesson.'

Comes back from court the next day and his wife brings him his sherry . . .

'You know that man you were going to fine £20 for being sick all over your jacket?'

'Yes . . .'

'Well, you'd better fine him another £20 – he's shit all over your trousers.'

MUSIC 'Let me call you sweetheart . . .
I keep forgetting your name.'

My very first guitar was a hand-made one, which I dearly
loved. Then when I was playing at a folk song club in
Dundee, I went out for a beer at half-time and when I got
back, someone had stepped on it! There was this great
commando-sole footprint on it, just like in the comics. We
tried to put it together again, but every time we did
something to one end, the other end would open up like a
sandwich. So some artist took it and it's on someone's wall
now.

The first guy I actually played in a group with was my
banjo teacher, Ron Duff. I really admired him an awful lot;
he could play great blues piano, folky, country guitar and
very, very good banjo. The last time I met him, he was
learning sitar and was very good at it. So it was a very
proud moment for me when I became the banjo player in
my banjo teacher's band. We didn't have a name for it – it
was just Mick Broderick, Jimmy Swankey, Ron and myself.

Then I met another banjo player called Jimmy Steele and
played with him for a while and he showed me a lot of
other new things.

After that, I formed a group called the Skillet-Lickers.
There were three of us: me, Jim Carey and George
McGovern – who went on to run for President in the
United States. Oh, he did well for himself, did George, lives
in Arran now. We were doing old-timey American music
. . . I stole the name from Gud Tanner's Skillet-Lickers.
Well, I didn't steal it, I borrowed it. He was dead, after all.

The Rue End Folk Club in Greenock was the place where I
had my first 'professional' gig, if you could call it that.
There was the three of us and they gave us a quid, so I got
six and eightpence. Great. We'd been rehearsing and
bumped into Matt McGinn in the pub and he said 'D'you
fancy playing at this gig I'm booked for?' – 'Sure.' So we
played the stuff we'd been rehearsing and it went down
extremely well. The guy handed us a quid, which was very
kind of him, since we hadn't been booked or anything.
I couldn't believe it, to actually get *money* for playing!

But the first *real* professional gig was in the Paisley Attic,
with Jim Steele, the banjo player. It was the first time I'd
actually gone out and played to folky people – it was
funny.

I disbanded the Skillet-Lickers and joined a bunch of
idiots, complete loonies, called The Acme Brush Company.
Nobody knew how many were in the band. If you wanted to
join, you just came along. If you knew the chords, you
played; and if you knew the words, you sang – it was that
kind of an outfit. I was the kazoo-player.

For a while after that I went solo. But I didn't like it very
much . . . I was playing mostly Appalachian and blue-
grassy stuff. And when I got fed up with that I joined Tam
Harvey and the Humblebums.

We got the name when Watt Nicoll suggested
'Stumblebum' and I think it was Tam who suggested
Humblebums; it's all a bit confused and lost in the mists.
Some of the disc jockeys never got to like the name, and
some of the press thought it was a bit rude, too. So we
would be called 'The Bumblebees' or 'The Humble Ones'.
Which was a bit narrow of them because as far as I was

concerned, 'bum' meant 'tramp'; it had nothing to do with 'arse'.

And while I was with Tam, somebody suggested to us that we get in touch with Tom Scott, who's now a friend, of Major Minor records, because he was auditioning people at the Trades Union Centre. Along I went. He told me I was good, but did I write anything? So I shuffled about a bit and sang my Song, my one song. He told me to go off and write another nine and send him a wire when I had.

Down to London I went. But Tom said he couldn't really fit that kind of music into what he was doing, so he sent us to some bloke at RCA Victor. But he wanted a 'pure country' sound and put us on to Transatlantic. But, well, I didn't bother. Until Bill Leader, another pal of mine, came up to Scotland to hear me and said: 'I think you're great and the band's amazing. Do you want to join Transatlantic?' So I did.

A wee while later I was doing a charity show in Paisley and Gerry Rafferty was in the audience. He came up afterwards and said that he wrote songs himself. So I said 'Great!' and thought, Yawn – another one. But he asked me to a wee do after the show, so I went along with him.

He sang his songs and, Jesus, I couldn't believe it. They were amazing, beautiful things. I said: 'Where the hell have you been?' He'd been sitting in the house for two years, doing nothing. Right away I asked him if he wanted to join the group. And I told Tam that there was this bloke who wrote great songs, played a lovely guitar and was an incredible singer, too. Can he join the group? Tam says: 'Why not?'

Just before that, Ally Bain had come down from the Shetlands and couldn't get work as a fiddler. So he jammed along with the band for a while until he got a name for himself and went on to form the various bands he's been in, like Boys of the Lough.

Gerry and I progressively disliked Tam's guitar. The more we were developing, the less he was fitting in. It was one of those unfortunate things.

So Gerry and I enlarged the group, to give it more beef, and we became a six-piece band – the shoddiest six-piece in the world. We had a lady organist, who was good, and a guitarist who came from Transatlantic's stockroom. The drummer was a great guy called Jimmy Something, but as a group we were a real unwieldy mixture.

At that time, I was still suffering from the delusion that I could write songs. Oh, they were rubbish: 'Looking into Your Eyes', horrible. And it was getting steadily more pretentious and trite. I had to own up eventually. It was getting more and more of a strain to go up on stage with this legendary singer-songwriter Rafferty and know that my stuff would just never match up. Even when I wrote a good song, he would tidy it up and it would become twice as good.

I think we both came to the conclusion that we had peaked as a band. And the more we went on, the further and further we were getting away from each other. So we broke up with the idea that I would try and get into theatre and Gerry would write songs and have a *real* rock and roll band, not a collection of window-cleaners and stockroom boys. So off he went and formed Stealer's Wheel.

In a way, I had the more difficult task because Gerry was already established and had a smashing reputation. But I was just known as a funny folky: I couldn't get into the theatre because I was too scruffy. And I couldn't get into cabaret because they didn't like folkies. It was very much a *Catch-22*: they wouldn't come and see me to find out what I was like and they wouldn't let me perform because of what they thought I was like.

Still, it was worth it. And I felt great the first time my name actually appeared on a poster. I think it was some kind of charity do, anyway, it was at the Woodside Halls with Matt McGinn or Clive Palmer, who was one of the originals in the Incredible String Band. They actually had my name on the poster and even in the paper to advertise the show. I was about fourth or fifth on the bill, but there it was: BILLY CONNOLLY.

Then once I had a few bob together, I hired a place and did my own concert . . . Musselburgh was my very first solo and I was rubbish. I discovered that I was awful bad on guitar, good on banjo. But I just couldn't accompany myself, because I was used to the band situation. So I thought I had better get better very, very fast or I was going to be a non-event.

I then came to the conclusion that the only way out of the folky bit was to put a beginning, middle and end to my act . . . so I reshuffled it, added some new stuff and called it Connolly's Glasgow Flourish. It was on for a year in Glasgow . . .

Spring has come
At last it's here.
It's been long gone,

Almost a year.
But here it is
And you can tell,
As stray dogs go
For walks themselves,
And pigeons murmur on the wing,
Oh, welcome, welcome, Glasgow Spring.

That was how it opened. And I did lots of freaking about
and pointing with fingers and stuff. I did it in the
Cumbernauld Theatre and it went down a storm. I said:
'This is it – I've got direction at last.' The news spread very
fast that I was a wee bit different, and it just rolled on from
there.

At the time, I had this manager-agent fellow called Dougie
Mitchell, who managed Larry Marshall, of all people, and
also a lovely man called Tom Buchan, the poet. I met Tom
in the office one day and we clicked right away.

So the first Clyde Fair International came along and my
manager said why didn't I try and do something a bit
different for it, and introduced me to Tom. And I said:

'OK . . . Look, I've got a title, *The Great Northern Boot Show*.
I want it to be about wellies and a sort of thinly-disguised
Upper Clyde situation, a work-in in a welly boot factory.
And I want to be the shop steward, Big Jimmy Littlejohn.'

Now I didn't know how to write a proper script, so that an
actor could just pick it up and go 'Oh, yes, I see . . . mmm
. . . Act One, Scene One . . .', but Tom did. So I wrote all
the songs and he did the script. The whole thing has become
a bit of a legend, though it was a bit of a disaster to begin
with.

Tony Palmer, whom I admire a lot, directed it – but it was the first time he'd ever done anything for the stage. And what with that and my amateurism and lack of discipline, it was a disaster on the first night. The week in Glasgow managed to survive, just, with very good houses, but we were just short of being laughed off.

Then I had this zany idea. I said to Tom: 'Why not take it to the Edinburgh Festival, hire a hall, do everything ourselves and everyone gets paid the same money?'

Tom was all for that; it could be us actually *doing* a work-in, as well as singing about one. And that's how the whole legendary bit started. We hired a ridiculous big arena, the Waverley Market, and built a theatre inside it.

Luckily, it caught the imagination of the Edinburgh public and it was jammed every night. A huge success it was, thanks almost entirely to Robin Lefevre, who reshuffled it and re-directed it properly for stage.

But the bit I was most proud of was when they had this post-mortem thing on television after the Festival: Why hasn't the Fringe worked this year and why was there no one at these shows? kind of thing. They were all flannelling about and Russell Hunter, who was on the panel, said: 'Wait a minute, not one person has mentioned the Welly Boot Show, which was a great success.' And this guy came away with an answer that I'll remember all my life:

'No – but that wasn't Official Fringe.'

That summed up the Edinburgh Festival for me in a nutshell.

Right after that I wanted to write Hamlet in my own way, call it *Hammy*, do it all in Glasgow and make it like a modern story. But I didn't get round to it, because suddenly my career took a real flip and I was a success as a performer and jamming halls everywhere.

I've had very, very few real bummer shows. But they were *real* bummers when they happened . . .

In Dundee, once, I was standing in for Hamish Imlach on a Watt Nicoll bill and I should have *known* not to do it, because it was that sort of northern-rugby-club-dirty-song kind of show. But I went along anyway. There was this halfwit in the audience who came up to me as I was about to go on stage . . .

'Do "Needle of Death", eh?'
'I'm sorry,' I said, 'I don't do it.'
'Aw, c'*maunnn* . . .'
'Look – I'd love to do it, but I just *don't know it*.'

I get up on the stage and in between every number that I do this guy is going '"Needle of Death".' As soon as I finish a song, this voice comes over: 'Do "Needle of DEEAAATTHHHHH".' Then someone at the back of the hall puts on the jukebox while we're still playing and I just about died on my arse. We were booked for half an hour and when the clock went Ding!, it was 'Thank you very much' and off the stage.

So I went down to the bloke and he says 'You didnae do "Needle of—"' WHAM! He never got the word out. I belted him, grabbed him by the collar and ran with him right to the back of the hall, dragged him into the office and socked him again. He was only the Treasurer! Three hundred guys in the place and I had to wallop the bloody Treasurer . . . he didn't give me a penny.

Another one was at Prestwick. It was the Annual Prestwick Somethingorother and it was still quite new then. I was booked with the Humblebums, Tam Harvey and myself.

They held it in this big open-air pool by the side of the sea. The audience was on one side of the pool and we were on the other. It was a complete disaster. We were playing some bluegrass music, with me on the banjo. But with the water being what it is and these open-air pools being what they are, Tam was getting kind of confused as to what was the echo and what was me playing. And after a while he was accompanying the echo. It must have been very confusing for our audience, because this guy was constantly one bar behind. Some of the time I would stop to listen and then start accompanying Tam, which was silly because I was meant to be leading. Then we would be together for a wee bit, then he would hear the echo and he would be away again, because he was hearing the echo better than he was hearing me.

Then in the middle of all this madness – this place was right on the beach, remember – the mist came in and blocked out the audience completely. And I would go:

'HULLOOOO . . . . ARE YOU THERRRRRREEEE?'
'YEAHHHH . . . . YEAAHHHHH'

So we would keep on playing. Then the mist cleared and I was completely fed up with the whole thing, so I just dived right into the water and had a swim with all my gear on. And we swam right over to see the audience. Matt McGinn, who was playing there as well, jumped in behind me and we all had a great laugh. And that was the end of the gig.

At Aviemore, in 1974, there were ten or twelve skinheads in the audience who were constantly haranguing me while I was trying to perform. They wanted me to do the 'Crucifixion' and I wouldn't do it for them. So from the start of the concert till when I walked off, it was Harangue-harangue-harangue. So I said: 'All right, OK, you win.' And walked off. The manager was a joke. He was frightened and didn't want to do anything.

And there were some plainclothes guys in the audience. They had been sent to various holiday resorts to wise up the local guys as to who were hooligans from Glasgow and who was to be watched. I think it all stemmed from Blackpool, the Glasgow Exodus to Blackpool on September weekends. There was always a vast amount of trouble down there, so the Blackpool police invited the Glasgow police down to point out the thugs. And they would just say 'Him! He's one', and they'd put the guy right back on the train to Glasgow. So these plainclothes guys were meant to be doing the same thing in Aviemore and the manager thought they would take action; but they weren't allowed to do anything until *he* did. So it all just got so horrible that I walked off.

Always, in these situations, the manager of the place will phone the press to get their story in first. Once it's printed, they tell you that they've contacted the press; it's a very sneaky, underhand thing to do. But not being the owner of the place, I suppose they get worried about losing their job. Luckily, there have been very few situations like that.

Oh, there was Banff, of course. That was a bummer. I knew that it was going to be a bummer when the manager spat in my face – I knew that wasn't a local custom. I really grew up in Banff – it took me about eight minutes. When we arrived, the audience were already outside, booing each other.

And while I was performing, they were all shouting at me: 'We cannae understand ye!' But I couldn't do anything about it, because I couldn't understand what they were saying.

Saturday night at the Aberfeldy Folk Festival was another one. I was shouted down. They just wouldn't listen at all, so I walked off. And I suppose I've had plenty of the Maybe-we-like-you, maybe-we-don't, and not much applause at the end . . .

Still, what are the three most unnecessary things in life? A nun's tits, the Pope's balls and a round of applause for the band.

Gerry and I played the Bilston Jazz and Folk Festival together. We were so nervous. Cat Stevens had just been booed off the stage, so Gerry says: 'We're not going on after *that*.' So they put on Atomic Rooster, who do a great set, and the audience are all leaping around, clapping their hands over their heads, HULLOO!

'C'maun . . . we can't follow *that*,' says Gerry.

'Well, who the hell do you want to go on after?' says the guy who's running the Festival.

Gerry looks round and sees these black guys from Holland or Belgium or somewhere and points at them. So on they go and play this *amazing* music. Crowd goes wild again.

'We can't do on after *them* . . . never, we'll *die* . . . no way . . .'

'Look,' says the guy running it all, 'either you go on now and play or you don't get any money.'

So we go on and I play 'Mother', which was my Solo Number, just me and acoustic guitar, with the band coming in right at the end. The crowd goes crazy, jumping up and down. So Gerry goes forward with his guitar, plays a number. Nothing. So he tells me to play another solo. But 'Mother' was all I had . . . oh, it was murder-polis all right.

One great mistake I made was when I was playing in a huge concert, *Stars for Spastics*, at the Kelvin Hall. I opened the concert with 'Cripple Creek'. Did I blow it! People thought I was trying to be funny, but, honestly, it never crossed my mind.

Another time I played at a mental hospital for kids, wee mongols. It was a huge success, once we'd realized that the lyrics of the song didn't mean a bloody thing to them. So I said:

'Wait a minute. Can anyone here dae the Twist?'
'Yeahhhh!'
'Right. We're going tae have a twist competition!'

So we played 'Let's Twist Again' and they're really giving it laldie. So I said:
'It's a drawwww!'

'Hoooraayyy!'
They were all happy about that. So then I told them:

'Right, we're going to have a *clapping* contest, see who can clap the best!'

And we played a lot of wee jigs and reels and stuff like that that was nice to clap to and they're all clapping away ...

'It's a DRAWWWW!'
'HULLLOOO!'

Then we played 'It's a Long Way to Tipperary' and got them all to put one hand on the shoulder of the person in front of them, and we marched through the grounds, in this long line, with them all hanging on to each other; they thought it was great.

Afterwards we went into this little bar to have a drink with the parents of the kids. They were all delighted ...

'Oh, I've never seen the children so happy ... you were wonderful, you're a genius ... it was splendid ...'

'Aye,' I said, 'and I really loved that clapping thing. Did you see the way they were all clapping away like *maniacs*?'

Silence.

I blame them for that; it wasn't such a grievous thing to say.

But one of my finest hours was in New Jersey, in this outdoor arena that seats eight thousand. I was invited to do a couple of songs at this Scottish Festival there. I got a standing ovation and it blew my bloody head off ... the guests were all coming on one at a time and getting clapped. And when I came on, everybody stood up and cheered and off went the top of my head.

And I've played in an open-air festival at Grangemouth, in a football ground. It wasn't exactly Woodstock, but I loved it. Christian – Chris McClure – was on the stage when I arrived and he just looked like a wee speck.

I love playing these big halls now, even though some of them are so bloody vast they look as though the Red Arrows practise in them during the day. Some of them are amazing places . . .

The Apollo at night can be very weird. There's a ghost in there, a guy who fell off the scaffolding when they were building it as Green's Playhouse. He's wearing a boiler suit and he's got bare feet because the scaffolders take off their shoes when they're working high up so that they don't slip. He got into the lift with the night watchman once. And one thing he likes to do is turn on the orange-juice machine, which he can do, even when it's unplugged.

The Caird Hall is an amazing canyon of a place, too. They asked me to sign the book there. The first person to sign it was Dame Nellie Melba – are you ready for that? I signed after the Queen Mother. She had signed 'Elizabeth R.' So I signed 'Billy C.' Bob Hope signed it in 1953: 'The first time I have appeared in a tunnel.'

I still have a lot of affection for the places where I used to perform when I was just starting out. I used to sing in a Polish Club – not a Polis Club, although they were around there a lot; in fact, I always seem to get a lot of policemen at my gigs, standing at the back with their wee radios going. But this was an odd club, it was near Sauchiehall Street, all those Polish guys eating weird Polish sausages and us pretending we loved their music and clapping in time to the Polish records so that they would let us keep on playing there.

That was where I met Iris, in fact. She was there with a friend of hers who fancied me and eventually ended up marrying my banjo-teacher . . . Marriage is a wonderful invention; but, then again, so is a bicycle repair kit.

When I was finally beginning to make it, all sorts of lunatics wanted to manage me. And I actually took one on.

He ripped me off *so* badly. One day I went into his office – this is just before I joined Unicorn – and he says to me: 'What you need is a cheque book.' 'OK, that's all right by me.' So I go down to the bank, blahbetty-blah, get my cheque book.

So then he tells me it would be simplest if I left it with him in the office. I don't know to this day why I fell for it.

And the next time I went into his office, he covered up this piece of paper he was writing on. Anyway, eventually I got a glance at it: he had written out my name about fifteen times, practising my signature!

What he would do is have all my returns sent to his office, then he would show me the stubs of my cheque book. And I would just go along with all and say 'OK'. I had no idea what was going on.

Finally, though, he was with someone from show business in Aberdeen and he was insisting on paying the bill for the meal, being the generous manager image . . .

'Oh, that's verra kind of ye . . .'
'Notatall.'

Signs the cheque. But the girl who was sitting next to him happened to see what he was signing – 'Billy Connolly' – and she told me about it. I've never spoken to him to this day, just once, when he phoned up:

'When are you coming into the office?'

'YOU ARE *JOKIN*'! FUCK *OFF*!'

Oh, I've met some right ones in the business. The folk club organizers. Eventually, when I wasn't getting any work, I wrote thirteen letters to folk club organizers, saying that I would play for just my expenses, provided they would book me if they liked me. I got four replies and that was really quite a crucial time for me, because after that I never looked back.

My appearance shocked a lot of guys. And the way I attacked the banjo – I really gave it laldie in those days. But they were very good about it; they never came up with suggestions or anything. They could hardly piss themselves laughing and then come up and say: 'This is the way you should be doing it.'

One guy I thought was an agent when I first met him was Jet Mayfair, who's become the sort of mascot of the Apollo – his real name's Stanley Frossman.

I was having a meeting with Frank Lynch and this guy
burst in the door, a wee guy with baggy trousers and always
lots of stuff in his pockets. I thought he was an agent or
certainly something like that, because he seemed to know
the business. So I asked him what he did.

He said he was a jet pilot. And I thought . . . Wait a
minute. Then he told me he had been in the Arab-Israeli
War and fought on both sides. And he had been the only
pilot in the war to wear a psychedelic outfit. So I said,
'Aye, that'll do me.'

Ever since then, I've had great laughs with Jet. He has
these amazing costumes which he'll dress up in and mime
to Elvis records at the discos. And he gets around. He went
into the dressing-room at the Apollo when Johnny Cash was
there and he was wearing a gold lamé suit. So Johnny Cash
obviously thought he must be someone . . .

'Say, what do you do?'
'I work the railroad, man.'
He cleans the signal lights on the railway.

And there's a great photo of him beside Diana Ross, too.
And Slade got him up on stage to mime with them when
they were playing in Glasgow. He was on one of my shows:
we had him come on and this giant finger pointed at him
and he turned round and on the back of his jacket was
WHO'S HE?

But in London the managers and agents avoided me like the plague. Gerry got lots of offers, because he's a very talented bloke. I never got any, because they'd never seen anything like me before. I wasn't a well-trodden path. Every gig I got, I had to talk the guy into it.

It pleases me greatly to have made it in London now, because I tried for many years when I first went solo and they would never even hire me, not even in the wee clubs or the folk clubs or anywhere. It was all:

'You're unknown. We can't book you.'

'Aye, but I'm tryin' tae get un-unknown – book me.'

Then they would offer me a fiver for the night, just silly Monopoly money.

It even got to the stage where I was busking, but never with an enormous amount of success, though I quite enjoyed it. In fact, I went busking in the Highlands and in Denmark as well, when I was over there.

But, funnily enough, I loved living in London. I was in Finchley most of the time and then we got skint and I took my wife back to Scotland to live with her mother. So I came back down on my own and stayed with a friend, Michael Campbell, at his place at the Angel, Islington; a real cold, wet place it was, too.

I remember very clearly walking home one night and seeing the slogan that had been painted on the wall there:

HANDS OFF CAMDODIA
Why not?

But I never looked on London as my home in any way.
I always felt, Well, I may be here for a few years, but . . .
I'm basically Scottish, and I think like a Scotsman and I
probably walk like a Scotsman. And I probably look a bit
'country' when I'm in London; apart from the clothes,
which are as trendy as anyone else's. But I could never look
on London as Home. I don't see how anybody can, except
for East Londoners. When you're living in the north or west
or any of those trendy bits in the south, it's not *your* home,
really – it's everybody's.

Not that I could live in many places in Scotland that are
far from Glasgow. Certainly I could never live in
Edinburgh. It's like a different world over there. It's not a
'people place' at all, it's a pretty picture. Obviously the
architects had a field day putting it together. I like what
that advocate Nicholas Fairbairn said about it: 'The people
of Edinburgh are like they are because they were all
conceived while their parents were fully clothed.' But I
don't count Leith as part of Edinburgh; I like it a lot, it's
just like Glasgow. Mind you, the Edinburgh audiences have
been extremely good to me, often better than the Glasgow
audiences, it's a strange thing.

I was attacked in the *Daily Record* by a woman from
Edinburgh and immediately all sorts of people wrote in to
tell her where to get off. That old battle between the two
places is always good for a line or two in the papers.

Touring is such an unreal world, but I do love it. It's tiring,
but then so are most of the worthwhile things in life. It

reminds me of when I was a kid and I used to take the day off school and wander round the shops. I had this feeling of doing what no one else is doing, and of no one knowing where you are.

Up till the last few years I never had a roadie as such, for travelling around with, like I have Billy Johnstone at the moment. Billy used to have a hot-dog stand in Glencoe and I would go up and see him when I still had my motorbike with the side-car on it. We would go into his lay-by and get some of his hot-dogs and tell everyone how wonderful they were . . .

'Hey . . . have you tasted these, eh? They're *fantastic* . . . . Mmmmm . . . . delicious . . . Oh, I must buy another . . .'

I've known Billy for ages. The day I asked him to be my roadie, I went down to see him at the yards, when he was working there as a spark. And the wee girls in the office were all giggling at me while I was waiting for him to get his wages and come out. He's a great person to be touring with. He keeps me cheery.

Before Billy, there was George, my Faithful Roadie. And before him, Ian Campbell. Except that he wasn't a roadie in the sense that George and Billy were, because he didn't get any money; he used to just enjoy coming along to gigs. He's working for Matt McGinn now – he must be giving him more than ninepence a week and all the programmes he can eat.

He was a tremendous bloke, he was deformed. He had this hunchback and he was very wee. And he was always making jokes about it, to the great embarrassment of strangers, and to my great amusement.

We would go into a pub and he would say to a bloke,
'Hey, can you lend us a quid to get straightened out?'
And people would look away and go 'Jeee*susss*' and I
would be biting the carpet, slapping my thigh.

Or we would pick up hitchhikers on the way to one of our
gigs. They would get into the back of the car with their
haversacks on and he would tap his hunch and say 'I
always keep mine under my coat – keeps it dry.'

And he was a great puller of women; he would get women
coming after him all the time. In fact, he was a far better
puller of women that I ever was. I sing this song about him,
'Song for a Small Man', which I sometimes wonder about,
if it's a wee bit sentimental for the act. But he likes it and
that'll do me.

So before all that, I spent years on public transport, which
was very pleasant really. I got to the stage where I could
stand in the bar of British Rail and there's all these guys in
civilian clothes – I could tell the soldier from the sailor and
the sailor from the airman. They all had a different look
about them, different kind of haircut. They wear trendy
clothes very badly, their flares are always too short. I used
to speak to them all the time. I loved that part of travelling:
talking to strangers, having a laugh, arguing, heavy debate,
drink. And there was always loads of drinking on the trains.
It was something I used to do a lot of, too, when I was in
the Terris – lurching down the compartments in search of
the buffet, bumping into all of the passengers and being
disgustingly rowdy.

I love just travelling through some of the places, the names still mean so much to me . . . Perth, where they have this Royal British hotel, and they would have just the initials of it on the wall: RB. And I used to picture it as a Rhythm and Blues Hotel . . . like you'd go inside and there would be all these black guys playing their guitars in the lounge and jamming away together. Can you imagine that, in the middle of *Perth*?

And Arbroath. That's where I lost my virginity. In a tent behind the graveyard . . . perhaps they'll put up a plaque there.

And all those places with weird names: Herbertstown – that must be full of wee herberts, all those guys who tell you that the quickest way to Doncaster via Norfolk is to take the A433, branch on to the sliproad, take the second left, *not* the first, although it's signposted, but the *second*, then cross the motorway on the flyover and turn straight into the B608 . . . God, those motorway bores.

Carlungie . . . sounds like a *disease*.

'Oh, doctor, I think I've got the carlungie. Is there anything ye can gi'e me?'

'Aye, here's a pot of black paint – put a cross on your door.'

And Husband's Bosworth! We drove through there on our way to watch the Ali-Frazier fight on the closed circuit thing in Leicester and I was delighted to see Ali win . . . but Husband's Bosworth! What a name for a place – it's down near Corby somewhere. It should be in a song, one of those ones that Steeleye Span would do, with one hand over the left ear . . .

A maid went to the market
In Husband's Bosworth town.
Her husband had been wounded,
By the Frenchmen been shot down.
'My lover has been laid low,
Shot down by a cannonball.'
They said: 'How much are your husband's ba's worth?'
And she replied: 'Fuck all.'

It's certainly a bit of a change, doing it all in the Mercedes.
They're amazing cars. I like what Frank Sinatra said about
them – typical German cars: power-brakes, power-steering,
power-operated windows, power-crazy.

There's this guy has a breakdown in his car on the motorway,
his tyre's got a bad puncture. So he gets out and takes the
wheel off, to change it. Another punter stops beside him,
opens up the bonnet and starts taking the battery out.

'What in the name o' God are ye daein'?'

'Well, if ye're goin' tae take the wheel, I'm havin' the
bloody battery.'

With the Humblebums, it was travelling around in a
minivan. There would be a continual argument as to who
should have the front seat beside the driver.

People say: 'Oh, that's terribly petty to talk about that
now.' But when you're on the road, it's *not* petty, it's very
important. Everybody should get a fair share. So if you sit
in the back on the way to the gig and your bum's sore, it's
only fair that on the way back, the other guy should sit in
the back.

A band on the road has to be awfully tight, mentally. You have to respect one another's ability. And it got to the stage with us that Gerry and I would be in one carriage of the train and Tam would be in another. And that's not on.

I liked playing as support band to a lot of people. We played with Hank Locklin and Tom Paxton and Pete Sarsted and Kenny Rogers and the First Edition. And, of course, with lots and lots of the folk people. I learnt a lot from them about how to conduct myself as a 'star', both on and off the stage.

I toured with Hank Locklin for a while. I thoroughly enjoyed that, because we used to play together and talk after the show and I thought we got on really well. Then he was playing at the Apollo recently and I went backstage to see him. And he didn't remember me, which hurt a bit, so I was just offski. Because when I was travelling with him, I was into the cowboy bit and I really liked his cowboy boots and he used to say: 'I may forgit ya, Billy, but my boots never will.' Then that happens . . .

Of course, it's exhausting, being on the road all the time. You get really knackered. I had pleurisy and pneumonia about eight years ago. There's no money in pleurisy. I had just run myself right into the snow, down on my hands and knees, being the Wild Raver. The light went out. And I had this uncanny feeling that I was going to die, because I was coughing blood all over the place, couldn't breathe properly, my legs wouldn't work. You have to be a bit careful in this game: that wee Marc Bolan had a heart attack, didn't he? And Jim Morrison died having a wank in the bath.

But you run into some funny ideas of stars on the road. The janitor at the City Halls in Glasgow was telling me about the time they had a big band playing there . . .

'Everyone says that thae pop stars have lots o' money,' he says. 'But it's no' true. See that band that was playin' here last week. There's *three* o' them and they're a' sharin' *one* roll-up! Honest – I saw it wi' ma own eyes.'

And you get to see a lot of new bands and hear new kinds of music. There are so many good bands around, particularly in America. The Eagles, the Flying Burrito Brothers, the Ozark Mountain Daredevils – what a name for a band, eh? And I love singers like Emmy Lou Harris and Linda Rondstadt. But I judge groups and singers by the sort of material they choose, not how well they play. A group could play 'Viva Espana' *perfectly* and it would do nothing for me. I hate that sort of song.

You get people like Steve Race going on about how rock and roll is just a noise, no skill, no talent. But look at the sort of music they were playing when *they* had the ball at their feet – rubbish. 'Love and Marriage go together like a horse and carriage.' Come *on.* 'Que Sera, Sera' . . . 'She Wore Red Feathers and a Hoolie Hoolie Skirt'. Where's that at?

I can't recall when I first started dressing up on stage or why. Somebody once said: if you've got their eyes, you've got 75 per cent of their attention. Which, I think, is a smashing thing to say.

I started off by wearing very, very gaudy trousers, with gaudy stripes, those American red, white and blue ones. I bought them in Maryhill Road in D. and M. Hoye, which was usually an extremely dull shop, all trench coats and sensible shoes. But they had this pair of jeans, which I just couldn't *believe*. And I started to wear them on stage and began to get a name for myself – 'Oh, my God, he wears the weirdest clothes' – so I started to wear other things and then WHAMBARAMA.

Iris started making me these very freaky trousers. She made one lovely pair that I wore when I was playing over in Amsterdam. I was walking over this bridge there, one of the hundreds of bridges they've got in Amsterdam, and this American bloke sees me. Now he's wearing these incredible leather trousers himself. So he stops me.

'Hey, man, where did ya get those trousers?'
'Ma wife made them for me.'
'Wanna swap?'
'Sure, why not?'

So we both take our trousers off, standing there in the middle of the bridge, and swap them. So off I go with this amazing pair of leather trousers, feeling really pleased with myself. Back to the wee hostel where we're staying, and it's one of those everyone-in-the-one-room kind of places. Somebody stole them in the middle of the night, some bastard ripped them off! So I'm left without any trousers and Gerry has to go off and buy me a pair of boring jeans.

Anyway, Iris was making these really outrageous clothes and people were loving it, they couldn't believe what they were seeing. At last, I had an Identity. Because, well, long hair and a beard was very original at first and people used to say: 'Look at the fucking length of his hair, will you?'

One folk club I remember was full up – it was the time when people were just starting to have long hair – and all these hippies rolled up and they couldn't get in. Tommy Cairney was running the show and he explained to them:

'Look, I'm sorry. We're full up, I'm afraid I just can't let you in.'

'Aye . . . it's because we've got long hair, isn't it?'

'Look – I don't care if you've got shite on your hair, but we're full up.'

I though that was a nice wee expression; because the place really was full up.

I had a full beard when I worked at the shipyards. But I burned it welding and now I've got this wee island on the right hand side of my face where the hair doesn't grow and you can see where the metal ran down. It was just a splash of molten metal and it went splooooshhheee – and the hair never grew again. It made me look all lopsided, as if I had a gumboil. So I took the sides of the beard off.

Tam's hair was even longer than mine and people used to shout at us in the street: 'Away and try a bath!' – I loved it. At last I was Joe the Somebody.

I wouldn't take my beard off . . . or at least there would have to be a very good reason for me to do it, like a good movie I was to be in. Then I would go into hiding until it all grew again. I've had it for ten years now without ever

As far as I remember, most of the time we were singing hymns

'And all you left-wing radicals don't give me any of your cheek
And start the revolution on a Saturday,
'cos I have tae work through the week'

Nights are fair drawin' in, eh?

'The British politicians, they havenae made a hit
They're ruinin' the country, more than just a bit,
If they keep on the way we're gaun, we'll all be in the . . .'

The man who Twisted for Scotland — and won

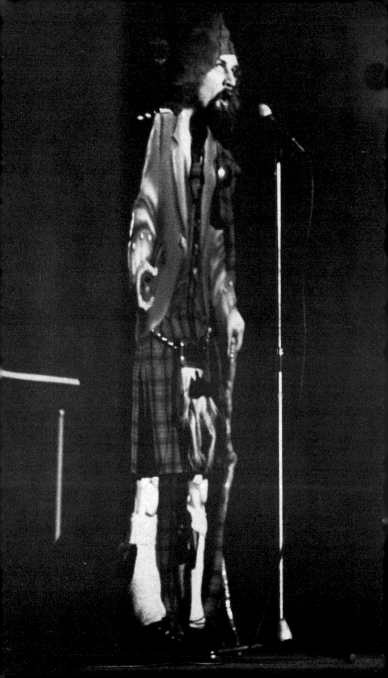

One singer, one song — eh? With (left to right) Jimmy Dewar, Alex Harvey, Jimmy Reid, Frankie Miller, and (front) Hamish Stuart

'SOOOROYALLL' (in English, 'It's our oil')

taking it off. One time I took the inside bit away and left an extremely long moustache and a wee bit of beard in the middle. But I looked devious in that kind of sneaky oriental way. I liked it for the one day and then I wished I hadn't done it.

What I really hate are those English guys with patches of hair on their cheeks; very southern counties, hunting-shooting types. It really looks awful, looks as though he's forgotten to shave. And then you look closely and say 'My God, he hasn't forgotten at all, has he?' I hate those rose-grower kind of mutton chops . . . those kind of guys who work in pubs in the south of England, the guys who play at being 'mine host', have them. They're usually the ones with the trendy wee horrible notes behind the bar – 'You don't have to be mad to work here. But it helps.'

I hate those clever-clever notes. The only one I ever liked was in a baker's in Govan Road, where we used to go to get broken biscuits and caramel wafers. The baker had this wee clock drawn on a piece of paper: NO TICK it said. It pleased me greatly.

Anyway, getting back to the costumes, I went from the stripes to the satin outfits, which were a wee bit fey, they didn't really work. They weren't outrageous enough, although the colours were nice. I had a scarlet one and a pink one, which worked very well; people would go: 'Oooo, give us a kiss' – and that was OK. And I had a white velvet one, too. They all worked in their own way, all did their thing.

Then I said: 'Time for an outrageous one.' So I got a floral outfit and a polka-dot one. And from there I've gone on to the tights and leotard, my Incredible Wilson suit. I don't know how women wear tights; they make all the hairs go the wrong way, so you're walking against the grain. And if you open your legs too wide, you get two wee lumps on the back of your head. Still, it's nice to have a gusset – I never had a gusset before.

One of the most beautiful things I ever wore was a jacket which John Byrne the artist painted for me with a felt-tip pen. It was amazing, quite amazing. I wore it on the Parkinson show.

John's an exceptionally talented bloke. He did my first solo album cover and he's done loads of book covers, for the Scott Fitzgerald books and all sorts of other things. He painted the mural that you see on the wall of that derelict building in the heart of Partick.

He signs himself Patrick, because one time he sent off his paintings to a London gallery and wrote in this very spidery kind of handwriting, and told them that he was a 63-year-old newspaper seller in Partick. They were amazed and they gave him a show. Then this young bloke rolls up and they could hardly say, 'Well, we don't really like your paintings . . .'

Another piece of clothing that I'm very proud of is Danny McGrain's Scottish international jersey, the one he wore when Scotland drew with Brazil in the World Cup in Munich. Danny's a smashing bloke, too, apart from being a brilliant footballer. And now I've got his jersey. I let people touch it, sometimes.

I wear an earring now as well. You can't often see it – it's a flying fish – because my hair's in the way. But I know it's there and that's good enough for me.

I had always wanted an earring. Robin Williamson from the Incredible String Band had one and I thought I would just have to get one, too. Then I read a British Rail poster about the origin of the earring in Greece: in order to get into heaven, the fishermen who drowned at sea had to cross the River Styx and give the ferryman a golden sovereign. But they were frightened that it would fall out of their pocket while they were at sea, so they had it made into an earring. I thought, That's really novel, I like that. And that was when it clicked that I should get one.

Quite a traumatic experience it was, too. It's like a tattoo. Once you've got it, you know you've got it. I wouldn't have a nose-ring, though. On a white person it looks like some kind of sore or blemish. I saw a girl in Glasgow with a ring through her nose. She was a white girl, a bus conductress and I thought That looks hellish, it really does. It was like a big shady wart.

But a wee man came up for an autograph in Aberdeen, a wee straight man. He was a fisherman and as I was talking to him, I suddenly realized that he was wearing two earrings. A fisherman from Peterhead or Fraserburgh, in his middle fifties – the suit, the neat shirt, the tie – and two earrings. He looked great.

Come to think of it, most of the people I know have earrings now, it's becoming quite the thing, isn't it. I took mine out for a while when the wee neddy guys in Glasgow started wearing them. But they soon stopped, so I put it back in again.

In London, when I was doing the Welly Boot show at the Young Vic, a guy came up to me wearing a single false eyelash and I thought that looked a bit silly. I've never been into the make-up thing . . . it was a weird time. One of the actors in the show was gay and when I was going on to do that song that starts 'I'm left behind, with you on my mind . . .', he would be going: 'I love your behind . . .' to the same tune.

But I did like some of the David Bowie make-up ideas and I admire that imaginative kind of thing. I didn't know him personally, but Gerry and I played at a club he had in Beckenham, called the Three Tons. He looked exactly the same as Bob Dylan in those days and sang like him, too.

I used to dye my hair a bit, too, blond at the front.

One time I was playing down in Hawick and I had put these streaks of silver in my hair – purely for effect, just sprayed it on. And I went into this fish shop for a fish supper after the gig was over and we were on our way back. There were a couple of Teds in there. They saw me, with my high-heeled boots and the long hair with silver in it . . .

'Are you a poof?'
'What if I was?'
So he looks at my hair.
'What's a' that stuff?'

And he leans over and pulls at my hair and the silver stuff comes off in his hand and then WHAMMM! He hits me and I go down and then it really starts. I wanted to kill him. It was a big fight, all rolling and kicking. Then the others come in to take me away and we get into the van with all the Teds chasing after us down the road.

So we lit up a joint in the van and I just felt awful. So I got them to stop so that I could be sick against a wall. And I was standing there watching myself fall and I was thinking:

That's . . .
Billy Connolly . . .
falling . . .
down . . . .

It was all in slow motion and I didn't feel a thing.

Aye, touring's great . . . all that indigestion and runs and boils and dirty hair and plukes . . .

AWAY Topless in Biafra, the Bears are Here Tonight in Vancouver & Snowy Mountain Daredevil

When I was seventeen, I got into this period of general frustration. I was fed up with the yards at the time, and the sort of nothingness of the whole affair. I started to imagine myself in the shipyards for the rest of my life, with just an occasional holiday. And I was just beginning to fancy seeing a few places, travelling about a bit. And I thought, God, you're just kidding yourself on – you'll never see anywhere, except maybe Spain for a holiday.

So I thought the Army would be just the trick. I went to the Army recruiting place and the Air Force place – I would have gone to the Navy, too, only I couldn't find their office. I decided I wanted to be a radar operator. I would have done anything to get away. I even went to the Merchant Navy, but it was overloaded at the time and they didn't want anyone new.

Once I'd decided to be a radar operator, I got the form, which has to be filled in and you have to name two people who will vouch for you, who aren't related to you. One of the people I put down was the local paper-shop man. And when he got the letter from them he went to my father and said: 'What's this?'

My father just talked me out of it in a very sensible way. He told me exactly what he thought of the Army and persuaded me against it. I still had this very romantic idea about the Army, especially the travel bit, like most of the guys of my age.

After I'd given that up, I saw an ad in the paper for the Snowy Mountain Project, in Australia. I was nineteen by this time and I pictured Australia as being the great land of opportunity, although I know there are a lot of very boring people there. Anyway, I filled in all the forms for this hydro project and sent them off, but by the time they all came back and I had to go and get a final medical, I had gone right off the idea.

Alaska was another place I thought about. I saw it on television but I never got round to any physical moves in that direction. The idea of Canada didn't really appeal to me and I thought I couldn't get into America, because I had a record. But I did want to go there very badly, and had a real airy-fairy idea of the place.

But they were all kind of half-arsed ideas. I never did much about them: got the forms and the brochures, filled them in and sent them away. End of story.

I suppose the nearest I got to Australia was building the *City of Melbourne*. It was a boat being built at Denny's yard in Dumbarton and the place had gone into voluntary liquidation. Stephens got the contract to finish off the half-built boat they had there, much to the chagrin of the local welders and platers who were on the dole. But there was nothing we could do about it; I was still an apprentice at the time.

I saw a really funny thing when I was there. There was a distillery next door called Ballantines, where they made the whisky. And I was out for chips at dinner time and saw a guy getting carried out of Ballantine's on a stretcher – he'd obviously been drinking the whisky instead of putting it into the bottles. From his knee down, his leg was hanging over the edge of the stretcher and he was all shouting and bawling and singing songs. And his insurance cards were on his chest! He was just poured into a taxi and sent away home with his cards . . . the Clydeside stamp album.

Eventually I did get to work abroad. I wrote to this company and told them that I wanted to do some overseas pipeline work and they sent me to Biafra.

My father had been in Africa during the war, so I was delighted to go, because I'd always, always had this hankering to see it. He'd been in Africa and India, for several years, and there were always the photos of the places he'd been, hanging around the house. I've not been to India yet, but I'm sure I'll go . . . I have this picture in my mind of myself eating an Indian royal banquet, the whole Ruby Murray.

It was only ten weeks that I was in Biafra, but I loved it. But I do remember the tragic sense of disappointment when we went into Port Harcourt one day, to go to this European Club. Not Welcome. We were just not the sort of European they were looking for *at all*. It was all British people, but they were very much the upper-class and middle-class consultant types. Being white wasn't enough to get in.

Anyway, I much preferred the black guys, although it was a strange time to be there: the war was on, although we were quite far away from it. It was up in Kano and we were down in Port Harcourt. After I left, it got awful bad – well, it's a legend now, the genocide side of things.

Just going there was one of the things that I knew was going to happen. Like the position I'm in now; I knew that was going to happen, too . . . you know you're a wee bit special, that you've got a special kind of talent, although it's difficult to pinpoint exactly what it is.

We lived right on the oil rig. It was the dormitory situation, the bunk beds, all very jolly. The local native guys used to bring beer up the river on those long canoes – you're not allowed to drink on the rig at all. It was great. They would come up with the Heineken and we would all sit in the barge, get drunk and watch these black African nights.

And I can remember watching two guys having this competition to see whose Bulova oyster watch was tougher and more shock-proof. Two guys standing there hurling their watches against a brick wall and then going and picking them up and seeing if they were still working. There we all are, drunk out of our heads, sitting watching them hurling their watches about. But you can very quickly get bored with people hurling Bulova watches at walls, as we found out.

Every now and then we would go into Port Harcourt. There was a club there called the Scoobeedoo. It was billed as PORT HARCOURT'S ONLY TOPLESS NIGHT CLUB. I went away in – it had no roof! That was the topless bit; it was their cooling system, I think. Anyway, it looked like the Colosseum. And there was me imagining this topless night club. I should have known better – they're all walking around the streets topless after all; it's no big deal in Nigeria.

Blue Band margarine used to be advertised out there in a big way. It was the time of the four little packs in a big foil wrapper. And they were advertising it in Biafra at the same time as they were in Scotland. Only, in Biafra, it was the mother walking into the kitchen, the kids with the big bright eyes, just like in Scotland – but mother was topless and the margarine was on her head!

Another thing they would advertise was this process for straightening their hair, which was very nice. Because they were only changing it so that they could look a bit different, and they were doing it for the right reasons; it certainly wasn't so that they could look like Roy Rogers.

America was another place I finally got to go to. But the first time I was there, I was only playing to Americans. It was dreadful; I was dying. But towards the end, I began to win heavily.

The second time I went, I played to Scottish audiences and I was hugely successful. On the third visit, we left it to a Scottish fellow who sold the tickets almost exclusively to Scots – I'd have been as well staying at home.

The first time I was there, in New York, I was wearing this fur coat, the earring, the dyed blond hair and the high-heeled boots. I asked this guy where I could pick up some fags . . . the look he gave me!

The American TV show is one of the most bizarre things I ever came across. The Talk Shows would be either super-safe or very schmaltzy, or else incredibly violent.

Johnny Carson had one of the Nixon men, Jeb Magruder, on his show. For some reason he didn't have to go to jail until after Father's Day, although he had already been sentenced. Very odd. Johnny Carson was asking him how he felt about the whole Watergate affair. And then he sprang it on him:

'What do you think about homosexual rape?'

The guy had obviously never given it a moment's thought, although it had been getting a lot of press in America, because of the White House men going to jail. The expression on his face was unbelievable . . .

'Er . . . I . . . er haven't thought about it very much.'
'Hadn't you better start?'
How do you answer that?

I've always found travelling round the States very strange. You keep arriving in places at the same time as you left the last place and you've always got the wrong clothes on. And then you're expected to get up there and play. Like at this Irish Club where I was meant to play for a crowd of decrepit Irish cowboys.

When I got to the club I was completely wiped out and I was meant to go on at half-past six. But there's not a soul in the club. All you can see are those little candles in glasses that they have in American night clubs. Just those and the barmen. At half-past six the manager comes over to me.

'You're on.'
'But there's nobody here.'
'This is America. You're on.'
Quite amazing. So I sang. And not even the barmen bothered to listen.

There are some bits of America I can't take at all. Like Los Angeles. Everyone is going around saying how wonderful everything is and how wonderful everybody is . . . 'I really love ya' . . . Phone-ey. I much prefer the madness of New York.

A lot of the exiles in America and Canada I find pretty hard to take. They're all more Scottish than the Scots and they love to tell you how well they're doing for themselves.

One of my friends emigrated to Calgary with his family – this is a true story. And he had to go through the whole immigration number, filling in forms and getting visas and photos and health certificates and vaccinations and everything. And the whole family had to give a urine sample so that they can be sure they're healthy enough to be allowed in. So his wee daughter has to give a sample and they have great difficulty getting one from her, but eventually, taps running . . . away she goes. They get into the car and they're driving back home and she's sitting in the back seat very quiet. Finally she says:

'Daddy, why did the doctor want my pee?'
'Well, he needs to test your urine.'
There's a long silence in the back seat, then:
'Daddy?'
'Yes?'
'Does he taste *everybody's* urine?'

In Vancouver, where I was for a while, they have this big thing that they're awful proud of: Civilization Stops Here.

There are these trees that you can see from the city centre in Vancouver and beyond that, it's all wilderness.

A guy was telling me, the day I got there, that an American couple had pulled in at a layby and there was a big brown bear or a grizzly bear or something like that eating away at the litter bin. And the couple got out of their car with their camera . . . the man was taking pictures and the woman was trying to manhandle – or bearhandle – the bear into the driver's seat of the car to get it to sit there and pose for a photo! It killed her and maimed him.

But there was a bloke from Drumchapel, Ray was his name, who was working in Nova Scotia or Newfoundland. He was staggering home one night, very bevvyed, with a bottle of Canadian Club in his pocket. And he comes across this bear that's woken up too early from its hibernation and is stumbling down this country road where Ray's working on the welding site. And Ray thought it was going to attack him so he belted it over the head with the bottle and knocked it out . . . the bear was out on its feet. And Ray got into terrible trouble, nearly got the jail, because bears are protected there – you're not allowed to get into the animals.

THE ARMY Officers & Scruffs, Firewater in Cyprus & the York Hill Draper

We got very little stuff on the war or the Army at school, because it was that weird time right after the war. Somehow the war was something they never really got round to talking about when I was starting school – it was around '46 and '47. We didn't even go into the First World War very much. They just taught us about all the little joke wars, the Floddens and Cullodens.

I don't really know why I joined the Territorial Army, but there was a guy at the shipyards who just said: 'Want tae join the Terris?' So I said: 'OK.' It was as quick as that.

So I went to the Parachute Regiment at York Hill Barracks. The regimental insignia was a footprint on your backside. But it wasn't like the real army, more like the Boy Scouts.

I make jokes about joining up because of the prestige and because I would pull women, but that was one of the reasons. The paras had this mystique, the Red Beret . . . you could always wear it to a fancy dress party with a yellow T-shirt – say you were a pluke . . . mouth full of custard. And the marine commandos had exactly the same thing, the whole heavy number, the Green Beret.

Anyway, the uniforms were awful, old Boer War outfits. Women used to come up to you and say:

'Oh, is that divided skirts come back in?'

And guys would give you money in the street; they thought you were doing it for a bet.

There was the whole spectrum of people in the Terris, most of them joining up just for a bit of adventure. And when you think of it – the first time I had ever been in an aeroplane was in the Terris. The first plane I dropped out of was the first plane I had ever been *in*. So it wasn't so much just a longing for adventure, it was just trying to do something I'd never done before, something as basic as flying in a plane. Aye, I fancied a slice of that.

I was six times in a plane before I ever landed in one. We were in this Hastings aircraft – they don't use them any more – and one of the engines died on us. I was delighted.

There were a few of us from the yards, but most of them were factory boys and a few clerks. I was in A Company, which was the rifle company: rifles, bren guns, machine-guns. It's funny, because I used to man a machine-gun post in exercises on this wee hill just near where I live in Drymen. It's weird driving past it and thinking of that figure in the Red Beret that sat there with a great machine-gun in his hands.

Some guys I know just joined to learn how to drive. The army driving tests are legendarily easy – nobody fails – and the licence does you for civvy street. So a lot of people joined up, passed the test and never went back.

Most of the officers had been regular officers; they were just middle-class boys. Except for Major Adam, who was in charge of the company I was in. He was a very nice bloke, had been right through the ranks in the regular army and become an officer in the Terris.

But it was all very definitely Officers and Men, even although it was just at weekends. There's a legendary story about it ...

When they were making the film *Oh, What A Lovely War*, they gave all the extras uniforms. Some of them got officers' uniforms and some of them got enlisted men's uniforms. And when they got them on, the officers wouldn't talk to the enlisted men! They were all extras getting exactly the same money! They even separated in the canteen, wouldn't sit next to each other.

And it was the same thing in the Terris: officers' mess, sergeants' mess and scruffs' mess. And if you misbehaved, made a right arse of yourself on a Friday night, you could be confined to barracks under close arrest until Sunday night. You went into this new world, just like being a regular soldier: you could be put on a charge, you could be fined, you could even be court-martialled!

My friends accepted me being in it because there was something kind of 'noble' about the parachute regiment. I don't think it would have been quite the same if I'd been in the Signals or one of the highland regiments. But the paras had this thing about them, the jumping out of planes was all quite romantic...

Somebody refused to go on one jump and they pulled him back into the plane. I was next. Then he changed his mind suddenly and jumped out. So I was just half-turning to ask the gaffer what's happening when he went: 'GO!' I went out sideways, twisted and hit the slipstream. And because your parachute's on a static line, I was like a yo-yo, being pulled round. So my head went dinga-dinga-dinga along the side of the plane. But because you're wearing your helmet, you don't feel anything. It's called 'ringing the bell'. Very weird experience.

The big off-duty number was going boozing. Get Drunk and Have a Ball. In uniform, of course. Do a bit of strutting in the Red Beret and your jacket with the wings on the arm. The wings were magic. And they would come in with a big truck at the end of the night and take you back to the camp.

In fact, the first time I ever sang in public was when I was with the Terris, at a place in Carnoustie called the Stag.

It had a lounge at the back with a big fat blonde playing the organ and rows and rows of tables. We all used to go in there at night for a bevvy. And they had a 'Go As You Please' – I love that term – when anyone could just get up and sing a song. I was more or less pushed and jostled up by my friends to go and sing a song. So I sang 'The Wild Side of Life', followed by 'I'd Rather Die Young than Grow Old Without You'. Why not?

I came off to a great reception because I had a nice high-pitched voice in those days. So there was this tremendous applause, everyone was delighted, including me. But it never struck me at the time that that was what I could be doing with myself.

We were in Cyprus for three weeks. It was all quite pleasant really. The real trouble didn't blow up until after we left; that was when the Turks sorted it out with the Air Force, about nine days after we had gone.

We got a lot of wee sneers in the street and people shouting things at us. It was OK really. Most of us were just intent on getting drunk. They gave us a little official sheet which said: 'The local drinks are OK, but stay away from *ouzo* – it is *firewater*.' So immediately everyone went: 'Right. Where's the *ouzo*?'

Another piece of advice they gave us I remember well. It was very cruel. It was on an official sheet, too, and it said: 'The only mysterious thing about Cypriot women is the diseases they carry.' It didn't say 'prostitutes', it said 'Cypriot women'. I thought that was a bit off.

We were given all the lectures about VD. And dope as well! 'You will be approached by different types of people who will offer you different types of things. And dope is one of them.' Nobody ever offered me anything! And they tell you not to say a thing about anything; you sign the Official Secrets thing on the day that you join. But I never saw a secret in my life. I don't think they tell Territorials secrets . . .

Just before Kennedy's assassination we were up in the Kyrenia mountains. There was a palace up there and I think it's the one they used as a model for Snow White or one of those Disney pictures; stuck right on the side of the mountain and we were just underneath it. It was very, very beautiful. We were fired at from the hills, but they were too far away from us to be effective – they couldn't have hit a bus from there. They were just some wee band of Cypriot rebels. I felt great about it!

Just after that a friend of mine in the yards went to Aden with the Terris, the Parachute Engineers, and got involved in real action, all firing at one another; one of their officers was killed. I remember being very jealous and thinking, God, I wish I'd been there. Because I was really pleased when I was fired at . . . it's funny how you change.

One of the reasons I eventually wised up was because there were just too many guys who wanted to see fighting and action and killing and a bit of the other, but without the hang-up of being a soldier all the time. A lot of them really fancied a slice of the action, or *said* they did. Whether they really did or not is something else altogether. But I know five or six of them who liked the idea so much that they went on to become regular soldiers.

I noticed that once they'd been in the Terris a wee while, they would start to get really interested in things military. They would buy magazines about the new guns that were coming out and the new advances in weaponry. But I was never like that. I never felt militaristic in my life.

Eventually I was just totally disillusioned with the whole number. It wasn't quite the voice coming down from the sky and saying 'What the hell are ye doin'?' But I was into my bike at that stage and I had lost some of the gear and been wearing bits of the uniform to work. So I paid the fine for the bits of uniform that I'd lost – they wanted to put me in prison – and got out.

They asked me to do a benefit for them recently after a whole lot of them had parachuted into a canal in Germany. I wouldn't mind doing something for them, not a benefit concert or anything, but I'd like to go up and just see what it's like now at the York Hill Drapers.

But it's funny. The more stuff I do about the Army on stage, the more you get soldiers saying how much they enjoyed the show. Iris and I were even invited out to Malta by the Army to do a couple of shows. They were going to fly us out and give us a holiday as well, with the kids.

It was like that with the police. When I was doing stuff about them in the act, they were delighted – even if it was stuff that was really putting them down. It was weird.

I drive past this new Army Information centre on my way into Glasgow. It's right beside the Broo, or the Job Centre as they call it now, it's really just a formica dole, a trendy Broo. And you'll see the queues outside the dole and the guys in the Army Information place beckoning with their finger:

'Come in, come in . . . come and work a computer . . .'

And you get some wee guy from Banff or somewhere like that, saying to himself: 'A comperputer . . . I think I could knock a tune oot o' one o' them, aye . . .'

The recruiting advertisements get more and more ridiculous, too. And I think the real cruncher is when they show you the WRACS. They'll have this film of them and they look right wee darlings. They're in Hong Kong or Malta or somewhere, sipping a martini and saying: 'I like meeting people.'

Have you seen the *real* ones? Oh-ho-hooo! Moustache and braces and a pint of Guinness. With all the charm of an Oxo cube.

I know the situation in Ulster isn't funny at all, but sometimes I'll hear a piece on the news and I can't help cracking up. When they say: 'A man was wounded in the Bogside', and you think, Hmmm, I wonder which side that is . . . or 'Wounded in the Falls'. That sounds *really* painful . . .

POLITICS The Reds' answer to Dr Finlay, the Patriotic Dinner Ticket & Bonnie Prince Charlie's Tights

I did a party political broadcast for the Labour Party in the 1974 election. And I'm very glad that I did it, although it was looked on at the time as being a very dangerous thing to do.

But Bill Simpson did one for the Tories and Leo Maguire, who wrote 'Leo Maguire's Song' that's on my album, did one for the Scottish Nationalist Party, but it was never looked on as being dangerous for them. Which gives credence to a thing that Jimmy Reid told me: that a vast majority look on Toryism as being the status quo and the rest as 'politics'.

But I was very happy to do it, because it was a very important election, the one that was brought on by the miners' strike. And I thought that if the Tories won that one, anything remotely to the Left could chuck it in for a good ten years.

The Labour Party camera team approached me. They were just passing by my house and they asked me if I would do it. And I said Yes. It was as quick as that.

The Tories were doing that Who Governs Britain? thing: the 'mob' or the 'democratically elected representatives of the people'. All that rubbish. You listen to the broadcasts of Parliament and you discover that the 'democratically elected representatives' are the real 'mob'.

I didn't look on it as being a vote for Harold Wilson at all. As far as I was concerned, I was doing it for the Labour Movement; that'll do me.

But I don't do much of that any more. It tends to dominate your life. You're held answerable for everything you say and it gets very, very boring. It gets *tragically* boring, in fact. I get asked to do current affairs programmes on the television as the Celebrated Man of Opinion and I avoid that like the plague, too. Partly because I'm a bit naive on the subject and partly because it's just not what I want to do. I'm no bloody crusader, God forbid – there's plenty of them around.

The Scottish Nationalist Party tended to assume right from the start that I would be on their side. A lot of young Scottish performers are SNP, in fact; the hairy, folky people tend to be a bit that way. They assumed I would be the same and kept inviting me to things, which I never attended . . . and all that sort of: 'Send us your favourite recipe for our SNP Cookery Book'. Jesus Christ!

What brought it all home to me was that the Scots I ran into abroad, in Canada and America, were all very SNP-minded. And I used to have a wee song called 'Stand Up and Fight for It'. But my line was very different from the SNP line. I fancied a wee Scottish Republic for very obvious reasons; because I like to think of myself as a socialist and I hated the fact that Scotland voted Socialist at every single election and then we got what England voted for. So I sang this wee thing:

If you love Scotland,
Stand up and fight for it.
Freedom is taken,
It's no' given free.

Sang it to all these exiles and I got the fright of my life. NUREMBURG! And I thought to myself, Wait a Minute!

126

So that one came right out of the repertoire and I never sang it again.

And Wembley when the Scots are down. I don't like that very much.

I met one guy down there the last time ...
'Are ye enjoyin' the gemme, Big Yin?'
'Oh, aye, we arra peepil ...'
'Were ye at HQ this mornin'?'

I thought it was some kind of bar he was talking about. It was Piccadilly Circus! They all gathered there and marched to the game like Bonnie Prince Charlie. A big bloody Exodus with all the thrilling music, amazing, astonishing.

I did go to see Scotland against Denmark at Hampden Park, though. That was OK. I was going to go on the pitch in my tights and leotard with a skull in one hand and shout:

'INTAE THEM, DENMARK! EASY, EASY! INTAE THEM, DENMARK.'

One thing I saw at that match was this punter that ran on to the pitch at half-time, dodged through the police, ran across the pitch, got away from all the police. And he's almost off and home safe when the linesman, who's wearing an orange jersey, grabs him from behind. THUMP! It would have to be an Orangeman to do that!

Those exiles that come up and tell you what a terrible mess Britain is in, I can't stand them at all. You run into them all the time in Canada and America. They come up to you and they always have to tell you how much they're earning – 'Very good, aye' – and then they get tore into the unions. It's all how the unions are ruining the country, holding the people to ransom. And then they tell you what a great life they're having. They're very welcome as far as I'm concerned.

Scotland will always be my home. I've no time for the 'stars' who say they can't afford to live in Britain. Sure, you pay a lot of tax. But you still have plenty left over to do what you want with. They're just greedy, that's all.

I have done various political benefits or concerts. I did some stuff for the Upper Clyde Shipbuilders, which I was very glad to do. And I did several Vietnam concerts, one in Glasgow on my own and one with Gerry Rafferty and the Humblebums in London. I've done some CND ones and gone on the demonstrations.

The Tories even asked me to do one for them – can you believe that? And Stuart Christie's people in London, Black October or Blue September . . .

But I sing my own stuff at them, not the anti-war songs. I did one at Clydebank when the Ban-the-Bombers were marching through Clydebank and they had been given the Town Hall to sleep in for the night. There was a wee impromptu concert and I went down to play there with Robin Hall and Matt McGinn. And I didn't sing any anti-war songs; it was the same when I was in Belfast, where I didn't sing 'Sergeant, Where's Mine', because I think it would have been a bit patronizing to sing to them about Ireland. I really didn't feel like subjecting them to something they knew damn fine themselves.

There are very few charity concerts that I feel like doing, because I don't agree with the principle of it. It should be a government responsibility. And I find it vulgar in the extreme when you go to one of those charity dos and they're auctioning things like a bottle of whisky:

'I'll pay £30!'
'Oh, *I'll* give £40!'

They're all wanting everyone to notice how generous they are. I find that amazingly tasteless.

If anti-militaristic people quote things that I have said or sung, that's fine by me. If I've said something, I'll stand by it. But I don't think I would involve myself physically in any movement.

Joining the union was an automatic thing for me. I liked the whole idea of unions and was very proud of being a union man. I got really irritated when we were up in Aberdeen on tour and the guy in the hotel is telling me what bad things unions are – and the people in the catering industry are the worst exploited of them all!

But it was great just belonging to the union, although the Boilermakers' Union wasn't exactly lauded in high places, even in union terms. No union men really liked the boilermakers – a bunch of scruffs and rowdies.

I thoroughly enjoyed all the union activities. Not that I got involved very much, but I liked speaking at meetings. It terrified me at first; it was like going on stage. I remember the first time I spoke. It was a DATA struggle . . .

The bosses had thrown the draughtsmen out of the yards; they refused to recognize this new union. So the draughtsmen were picketing, which was very strange because they always kept well away from the black squads, kept themselves to themselves very much. And there was a big meeting about whether or not we should support them. Most of the guys were against it because they never helped us: 'When did they ever give us any money, eh?' It was all: 'Those bastards up the stair with their white collars and their mincy fuckin' walks – when did they ever dae anything for us? Never look at us in the street, far less gi'e us any money.'

This was the first time I had ever spoken at a meeting. I said it was an attack on Trade Unionism, not an attack on DATA. And I sincerely believed it. It raised a few titters . . . 'Oh, look who's talkin'' . . . but I was very sincere about it, a bit desperately naive. Anyway, we supported them.

The main battles were always about money. We worked on piecework – the more you do, the more you get. But there was a ceiling on how much you could earn and we were always trying to get that ceiling taken away. And I think the Clyde should have got rid of it; the production would have been amazing.

It was a false economy not agreeing to it. 'We don't want to give them too much money.' Why? We were doing the work and they were setting the rates. But they kept the ceiling so we were always fighting against it, or to get conditions changed, or to get bonuses. Like we were always having to clean up – you'd do a welding job and it would be filthy, so you'd have to do all the cleaning up first. So you'd say: 'I'm a welder. I'm no' a cleaner.' You want the job prepared when you get there. It was always these continual struggles: 'Hit the pavements, lads, TARANTARAAAA!'

The Apprentices' Strike was the first one I was ever on:

Two, four, six, eight,
Give the boys a higher rate!

Which strike, incidentally, was led by Gus Macdonald, who was an engineering apprentice in my yard and who's now Executive Producer at 'World in Action'.

The journeymen very rarely took the boys out, though. But I remember one occasion very clearly when the apprentices were called out. Oh, I was so proud. But I wasn't proud when I got home.

'On strike, are ye? Laziness, I call it . . . work-shy lout . . .'

My father didn't mind so much. He just thought it was a bit off, hauling out the apprentices. But the men were right. As soon as they were out of the door, the bosses were getting the apprentices to do the men's work. Oh, I felt really adult then.

But it did get out of hand sometimes. You could have a real bummer of a shop steward.

I had one when I was in John Brown's, in Clydebank. Twelve weeks I was there and I didn't have a full week's work. I didn't mind hitting the street, but, for Chrissake, nothing was ever solved! You always went back in exactly the same position. You'd have a meeting outside: 'Right, lads, let's take the rest of the day off. That'll show 'em.' But it *didn't* show them. And then you might have lost four hours. And if you'd worked on the Sunday, that was all your overtime blown. It blew out all the good of getting up on a Sunday morning, the extra money was gone.

The relationship between us and the employers was non-existent. There was no mixing, no Christmas or New Year Party. Absolutely hee-haw nothing, except for the Boys' Club. No gifties, no pressies . . . and I used to see those American movies – there was a big era of goings-on-at-the-office movies, and those office parties looked so good . . .

Jimmy Reid got asked at a Glasgow Council meeting why he was down in London watching my show at the Palladium in January 1975, when he should have been on council business or at the meeting. But it was just them trying to stir things up. The show was on a Sunday for a start, so there couldn't have been a meeting. And anyway Jimmy told them that watching Connolly was therapeutic and watching the Tory councillors was positively masochistic . . .

I am a member of Equity now and I've actually been invited on to the committee. But there's not a lot of full-time showbusiness people up in Scotland and all the action seems to be going on down in London, with Vanessa and that . . . she came to the show at the New Victoria with a big bag of mussels; the place smelt like piss. I told Billy to give her a ticket but keep her out of my way.

Now that I've got a bit more free time, I think I'll involve myself in the union a bit more. There's a few things I'd like to see changed: the ridiculous money that's paid to dancers, for a start. When there's a guy at the top of the bill getting paid thousands of pounds and they're giving the dancer £20, and £5 or sometimes nothing for rehearsal – that's just not on. And I'd like to see actors getting to do all the advertising work on commercial radio, instead of the DJs, who I don't imagine belong to any union.

My family weren't much interested in the Queen or the Royal Family. But I remember the great furore when the Coronation was on, because that was the advent of television as well – Television for the Masses – and we all crowded into a house together to watch it.

My one memory of the Queen was when she came up to open some dam or hydro-electric project and she was passing through Glasgow on the way, going up Kelvin Way in procession. So they let all the schoolkids out to see her and I was one of them. I would be about ten and I had no money – well, like most schoolkids had no money; and she was coming up the road in the limo and all the kids were waving flags. And I didn't have one!

But I had my dinner ticket for school, this bloody dinner ticket, so I drew a Union Jack on the back of this wee rectangular dinner ticket. I drew the lines in, just like a Union Jack. And there were a lot of bushes and trees and things in Kelvin Way, so I got a wee branch and poked it through my dinner ticket and waved it at the Queen, thinking I was being a great patriot.

The Duke of Edinburgh came to the yard once. Oh, it was hysterical. They cleaned up the dump: they had this bizarre scrapyard, which was full of scrap that could be used again – you could go and cut a piece off to use as a stanchion, kind of temporary stuff. But this mass of metal was lying around all over the place and they tidied it all up. It must have taken weeks. Then they laid this sort of grass stuff down, instant lawn, and painted white lines through the workshops and said that no materials were to project beyond the white line – incredible.

We were all given a boiler suit with a Stephens badge on it, except for the welders; they were given a badge for their leather jackets. And as soon as the Duke had gone, the grass was taken away, the scrap was put back, the white lines all deteriorated and disappeared, and we had to give all the badges back! But the badges were glued to our leather jackets and when they were pulled off, bits went flying off them; they were totally useless, but they still insisted on taking them back. It left a wee circle of glue on the jacket . . . the whole operation was quite amazing.

In Catholic schools you don't get much of the monarchy bit. When you're singing, it's usually the Jesus thing. The Queen number was there, certainly, but never a big thing. I was a Scout, of course, and she was part of that, all right, but that was the nearest I ever came to it. Nobody ever shoved it at me.

Almost everyone I knew kind of disrespected the Queen. Most of my pals at school were of Irish extraction and there was no great patriotism flying around. My own father's parents came from Galway – my mother's were from the Western Isles – but I've never bothered too much about my ancestors. I can't see the point in it. They're all dead anyway, aren't they? And I've met so many tragically boring people who have done it.

But I would never take a knighthood or any of those decorations. I mean, can you imagine it? It would be selling my punters out completely.

What we did get on Royalty at school was the whole Bonnie Prince Charlie and Mary Queen of Scots number. But the Catholics got different history books from the Protestants, different slants on people like Henry VIII. Mary Queen of Scots came through very well. She was almost a saint! Bonnie Prince Charlie was a biggie, too, being a Stuart. Because we all knew that the Stuarts were lovely folk.

They didn't tell you that he was queer, though, or undersized, with a lisp. It's a shame, that. Have you ever seen his trousers? Oh, Christ, they're in this wee museum in Fort William. It's right on the main street, at the little square by the town hall. People often walk right past it, because there's no advertising or anything. Which is a sin, because there are some incredible things inside: those Jacobite drinking glasses – the base of the stem has got splodges of paint on it, it just looks as though someone's been doodling with a brush on it. But when you turn it with the light in a certain way, the reflection in the glass is Prince Charlie . . . And they've got these trousers in a glass case that belonged to him. And he was a tiny, tiny bloke. They're faded tartan trousers and they're really like a pair of tights – they've got feet. They're very baggy-saggy arses, really funny-looking things.

The history we were taught was very much a British affair. There was no slant in it that Scotland had been messed around in any way. And I must admit that towards the end of Charlie, Prestonpans and stuff like that, he did look a bit of an eejit, no matter how much they tried to cover up for him and gloss it over.

We got very little on John Knox, either. Except that he was evil – evil and dull and boring. Which I believe to this day.

I watched all three of the Party Conferences on the television in 1975; they came in the middle of the tour. I found them all quite frightening. One thing you don't hear a lot of at these conferences is a regional accent; there don't seem to be too many of them around. And they would keep bashing the table, and never quite hitting it at the right time, for the emphasis they were trying to make.

What really did it for me was when the Tory candidate for Walsall North, Stonehouse's constituency, told us that the best-off workers in the country were lavvie cleaners. Are you ready for that? All because they could work a certain number of days and still claim their Social Security.

Not that I approve of people sticking indefinitely on Social Security, if there is work around. Fair enough if you can't get a job. But if people get on to it when they can work, it gives Margaret Thatcher and her kind – oh, Margaret Thatcher, that voice and those wee fascist eyes – it gives them a perfect opportunity to attack the Welfare State. And I happen to think the Welfare State is bloody great.

I was on Social Security one time and I went along to the office to get my money one morning and they refused to give it to me. Do you know why? The previous night I had done a charity show and one of the guys working in the broo had seen me there and thought, Hey-hey, wait a minute, this guy must be earning some money if he's up there on the stage. And I was doing it for nothing! But the bastard refused to give me any money. So all I ever got from them was £9·60.

There's a lot of good stories about the broo . . .

This guy goes along to sign on one day and he asks the man if they've got anything going.

'Aye, there's a job up at Calderpark Zoo. Get over there, eh?'

Off he goes and finds out that he has to clean out the animal cages. Very good. First of all, he has to go off and clean out the tiger's cage, then the elephant's, then the lion's and finally the octopus's aquarium . . . Great animals, octopuses: they can pick their noses and scratch their arse at the same time. Anyway, he does all the cages and goes round to clean out the octopus's place. The keeper in charge of the octopus is there.

'Now what ye have tae dae is very simple, pal. Just empty oot the dirty water, take oot the octopus, clean oot the pool, fill it up wi' clean water. And then put the octopus back in. OK?'

'Oh, aye, very good.'

So he takes out the octopus, empties out the water, cleans out the pool and fills it up again. Goes to get the octopus, to put it in again. Looks round for the keeper, but he's away playing cards, so he reckons he'll just have to put it back in on his own. Tries to pick up the octopus and it's right on to him, arms and legs all round him, tentacles everywhere, grabbing him. No use. Finally disentangles himself and goes off to find the keeper.

'Hey, I cannae get that octopus intae the pool. Every time I try and pick it up, it grabs me wi' its airms and I cannae dae anythin'.'

'Oh, Jesus,' says the keeper. 'You dinnae dae it like that. You use a bloody *shovel*!'

'Oh, a *shovel* . . . aye, very good, right.'

Off he goes, gets the shovel and tries to shovel the octopus in. But as soon as he gets the octopus on to the shovel, it's right round him with its tentacles grabbing him everywhere, round his arms and neck, until he has to throw it down on the ground again. Back he goes to the keeper again.

'Hey, I just tried wi' the shovel and it didnae work. Whenever I tried tae pick it up, it would crawl roond the shovel and grab me . . . I'm awfie sorry . . .'

'Oh, ferheavensake, I'll show ye how tae dae it masel.'

Off he goes with the keeper. So the keeper picks up the shovel, right up above his head and gets ready to belt the octopus. The octopus sees him, whips all its tentacles round its head to protect itself and WHAM – he slides the shovel under its bum and wheeches it into the pool.

I've had lots of enquiries about going to South Africa to perform there. I was wondering whether I should or shouldn't. But how can I refuse to go to South Africa and then go to America?

I'm in a weird position because I'm Scottish and my act is intrinsically Scottish, so I wouldn't be playing to the Bantu guys at all. I'd be like a Chinese poet in Glasgow. I'd have to give it all a great deal of thought and introspection to do what I thought was right. And there's a lot of people refuse to go to South Africa, I feel, without being asked to go in the first place.

A lot of Scottish footballers go out to South Africa when they've finished their careers here. There and Hong Kong. Wee Willie Henderson, the Rangers player, is out in Hong Kong and he says he likes it, because he's big there. He'd never been a big bloke in his life before, till he was there.

I'll not go to Singapore. They don't let you in with long hair and I'm certainly not about to cut it for their benefit. But they would let Ronald Kray in with his sort of hair. Or wee Adolf. He always had nice neat hair, trousers always pressed, shiny shoes.

Yes, I'd like to get something funny on Hitler. And Stalin – I think he's ready for a joke . . . I can't take it the way the Left is all split up, getting caught in the little intellectual points. They did that in Spain, for Chrissake, and wrecked the whole thing – the International Brigade got split into factions and got fucked.

But there is one about Stalin . . .

Stalin and Churchill and Roosevelt all met at Yalta for their famous conference. And they're all still a little nervous and suspicious of each other, checking each other out. Halfway through the meeting, Stalin spots Churchill pushing a note with his foot under the table to Roosevelt. So he grabs it. And he's *furious*. Picks it up and reads it:

'THE DEAD BIRD NEVER LEAVES THE CAGE.'

So he thinks, Wait a minute, they're passing messages to each other in code. So he calls in his interpreters and the Russian code-breakers, all the experts, gets them all to work on it. And they're studying it desperately, trying to break up the code and find out what it means. But after a few hours, they've come up with nothing.

So Stalin waves the paper at Churchill and says:

'Well, we've got the message here so you might as well tell me what it means or the conference isn't going on.'

'I was merely replying,' says Mr Churchill, 'to a message that was sent to me by Mr Roosevelt.'

'Oh – and what did Mr Roosevelt say in his message to you?'

'Your fly is undone.'

RELIGION The cold wind from Geneva, the Saffron Tractor & 'Nae other Gods; Ah'm the gaffer'

I've always tried to avoid the crusader aspect of things. I don't want to be a teacher: 'I know the Truth and Here It Is . . . Good People of Glasgow, you are going Wrong' and all that kind of garbage.

Even the people who practise the heavy Catholic-Protestant bigotry, they *know* they're wrong, but they *like* it. It's like smoking: if you like it, you just get on with it, even if you know it's bad and everyone tells you how bad it is. And, anyway, it would need someone bigger than me to tackle the whole thing properly.

What's happened now is that I've become very associated with attacks on religion, even though there was hardly anything about the church in the last show I did. I have nothing against religion; well, I have lots of things against it, I suppose, but I feel that it's big enough to defend itself.

You look at all the money they spend and the great big churches and stuff and then people tell you it's wrong to attack it all. Why? They don't tell you it's wrong to attack politics, do they? Why is religion so special?

Anyway, I find religion incredibly funny. The language they use and the clothes they dress up in. All those bishops with the funny hats and the wee lacy bits and cuffs and collars, how can you not laugh? And all the titles and things – the Pope and the Moderator of the General Assembly of the Church of Scotland. I think it would be unnatural not to laugh at them and I think it's very healthy when people do. In fact, it would be a lot healthier if all the people in the church laughed at themselves a wee bit more.

Because look at the power some of the churches have. Up in Stornoway, there was this place that was serving drinks on a Sunday. So the church gets tore into it, tells all the congregation that if they want to be married or christened in the church, they'll have to stop going drinking in there at all, not just on the Sunday:

'Drink in there and your wains don't get christened in here!'

Then the minister tells them that they shouldn't even buy things from the shop of the *brother* of the guy who runs the hotel. That's 'sinful' as well. So they drive them out of business. Meanwhile, all the punters from the church are nipping in there for their Sunday drinkipoos. Oh, no, they wouldn't go in during the week, but when there's nowhere else to get their bevvy on a Sunday, they peep round the corner to make sure no one's watching and then – in. It's all so hypocritical.

And I hate the solemn bit about it all, that you get in Scotland. If you listen to a service in a black church in America or Barbados or wherever, they're all having a really good time, singing these beautiful songs and really enjoying themselves. Some of these big black gospel singers are just a knock-out. One I remember seeing who was singing away and took a mouthie out of her bra – she had one of these big enormous bosoms – took her mouthie out and really gave it laldie. You never get that sort of good time in the churches, and you should . . . I love all that 'Operator, Operator, get me Jesus on the line . . .'

Funnily enough, I was quite keen on the whole religious thing as a child and there were always the pictures in the house and everything. I thought Catholicism was lovely.

And it *is* quite a pretty thing – the incense and the music and the whole number. In fact, I was one of the Children of Mary, I was that into it all.

I drive past the churches sometimes on a Sunday, maybe going for a drink. And I have a wee smile when I see them all outside in their smart wee coats and the handbags and the neat little shoes. It's not the worship that I'm attacking, it's all the stuff that surrounds it.

What I object to with a lot of the people at the top of the church is the way they're so cautious, they don't like to discuss the really important issues out in the open. I would like to see the Moderator of the General Assembly of the Church of Scotland and Jimmy Reid have a discussion. And the things they were doing to him when he was running for election to the executive of the AUEW!

There would be people going round the Protestant homes telling people not to vote for Jimmy because he was a Catholic. And others going round the Catholic homes, telling them not to vote for him, because he was an atheist. And one minister telling people from the pulpit not to vote for him, because he's a communist!

You can never really get into a real discussion with a lot of them. Like that old question that always comes up about 'How can there be a God if people are always suffering and fighting and dropping bombs on each other?' But they won't answer it, because they've heard it so many times before and they think it's a naive kind of question to put. But it's not. It's a very basic, essential thing to want to know.

When I was doing the Crucifixion piece, the Last Supper number, there were many occasions when people really disliked it. And they're quite entitled to dislike it, that's fair enough.

I was even punched once. There was this Jesus Freak, oh, he had all the patches and badges and gear on – 'Jesus Saves . . . Jesus Loves You', the lot – and he got really angry about the Crucifixion. Fortunately I have this very long beard and my chin doesn't go down to the end of it, because he punched my beard! WHOOOOSH. Missed my chin and never connected.

But the people who liked it vastly outnumbered the ones who didn't. And it was often the religious people who would come round afterwards and say how much they had enjoyed themselves, which was great. It was the lip-service Christians who disliked it and voiced their opinions about it.

Even when you do try and attack religious bigotry, sometimes it just doesn't work. I did a piece once about the Orange Marches and how mad they all were and this guy comes up to me afterwards.

'Hey, Big Yin, that was great the way you got right intae thae Catholics.'

He thought the whole thing was an attack on Catholics. You just can't win.

Then in September 1975 I did a piece for the Religious Affairs programme at the BBC in Glasgow. And all the people running the programme were very happy with it. It was just a short piece with me in a dog-collar doing a Glasgow translation of Moses in the bullrushes. I bought a wee child's book on it to get all the details and it's amazing how violent it all was: 'Kill three thousand of them.' And I finished up with the Commandments:

Nae other Gods; Ah'm the gaffer
Nae knockin' stuff
Nae doin' each other in
Nae workin' on Sundays, double time or no
Nae fancyin' yer neighbour's wife or gear
Nae shootin' a line

It was all quite simple and not very offensive at all. And I did a wee interview afterwards with Cindy Kent about what I thought about religion.

Then the next day there's this demonstration about it outside the BBC. All these wee men walking around with placards:

GODLESS CONNOLLY
CONNOLLY THE BLASPHEMER

And they're led by this very odd wee man called Pastor Jack Glass, who is always around on these sort of things. He's a sort of watered-down Ian Paisley. He even sells Protestant papers at the Rangers' games at Ibrox, he's that keen on it all. I wrote a wee song about him once to the tune of the Rolling Stones' 'Jumping Jack Flash'. It went 'Pastor Jack Glass is an ass, ass, ass . . .'

Of course, he knows I'm a Catholic so that doesn't exactly help him to love me any more. He once stood for the Protestant Ratepayers' Association. What a name for a party, eh?

I have been to parties where the hostess is a Catholic and she'll tell you how unprejudiced and unbigoted she is. Then you look round and see that there's nothing but Catholics there. But, on the whole, the Catholic Establishment in Glasgow avoid me. We really parted company quite a long time ago. I think I've become more of an embarrassment to them than anything else.

But what gets me most about the Catholic Church is people like Franco. What did the Catholic Church ever have to say about him? Where's all the opposition from the Church in Spain to what he did? Why weren't all the voices in the Church raised against him, instead of helping him along all the time?

And what was the Church doing about Mussolini? When it comes to the crunch, the Church are always missing, they've got nothing to say. They're very good at making little speeches when there's nothing at stake, but they never come right out and commit themselves when some animal like Franco is doing things to people.

All this business about the Americans having found their first saint I find quite hilarious. All of them going over to Rome to celebrate. They were selling posters of Oliver Plunket in Dublin when I was there, too.

One thing I've never been to is one of these big Billy Graham rallies, just to see what it's like; I think it would be quite fascinating. But I couldn't go along now without someone recognizing me and being in some way identified with him, which obviously is not exactly what I would want. But I would like to see him in action – I imagine it's quite frightening when he gets up steam. I don't like all that coming forward in wheelchairs bit. But Johnny Cash and

Cliff Richard are right into that. And Hank Marvin's a Jehovah's Witness . . . very odd.

I did have some Jehovah's Witnesses round at my door a few weeks ago. Quite amazing. They were beautiful, nice young women, whereas your average Jehovah's Witness is a dried-up sort of creature.

They're amazingly persistent people, too. They won't take no for an answer. I was working in the power station in St Helier in Jersey a few years ago and some of them came to the house we were staying in, to try and give away the pamphlets and do their patter and everything. I couldn't get them to go away, they couldn't believe that I wasn't very interested in what they had to say. So I swore. I didn't swear at them or anything like that, it was just:

'Oh, is that one of your pamphlets? Let's see it – oh, that's fucking great. Hey, is that right, eh? Fuck me – I never knew that . . . fuckin' amazin' . . . Oh, aye, very good . . .'

Off they went. Then I'm back upstairs and I hear this strange sound coming from somewhere, a sort of kissssshhhh, kissshhhh. I looked out and what they were doing was making all their wee bible tracts and pamphlets into the sort of paper aeroplanes you make at school and firing them into the house.

Some of the other religious factions I'd like to get tore into some time: the Hare Krishna and the Jesus Freaks and the

Children of God and the Guru Maharaji. And the Maharishi – he's getting trendy again.

I never had flirtations with any of them, but I flowed along with the merry throng in '69 and '70: the interest in the eastern thing, the sitar and the Maharishi. I toyed about with the Bhagavad Gita thing, on the fringes, and then I just got very bored with the people involved. They all had that sort of imbecilic smile that the Hare Krishna have got. So I thought to myself, Get out of here or you'll be getting your hair cut. Those Hare Krishna haircuts – that's what I call a real sacrifice.

The Hare Krishna thing disappeared quite quickly in Glasgow. And I'm sure if I'd been one of them, my arse would have just been a blur on the road to Edinburgh; they're a lot easier tolerated over there for some reason.

I can take the Tibetan monastery in Dumfriesshire. That's old enough and hard enough to be real, or at least real for the people involved.

But then the sacrifice that the Hare Krishna people get into is quite heavy as well. Apart from the haircut, there's all that silly gear that they have to put on: the long johns, somebody's curtains, the Hush Puppies.

They all seem to walk kind of funny, with their little scrotum protector, the anoraks – and saffron robes just weren't designed to have anoraks worn on top of them – and the balaclava! I gave up wearing a balaclava when I was a wain and I've no great desire to go back to it. It's a cartoonist's dream, the whole outfit:

'Sure I like what ye're sayin' – but I'm no' wearin' that gear!'

And they've got bad teeth as well, very dirty teeth, for some reason . . .

I once had a lovely magazine that I got from a guy in the street in Toronto. It had a picture of the Hare Krishna factory in it: they're all going about on saffron tractors, saffron fork-lifts, with saffron crash hats on and saffron computers, which were programmed to go 'Hare Krishna, Hare Krishna . . .' It was coming out all the time, all night when they were in bed, it would be going 'Hare Krishna, Hare Krishna.' And that record they made of it made them a lot of money. But the bit that got me was when they made the follow-up record, 'Govinda' – they got session men in to do it.

I don't think the wee fat Guru ever came up to Scotland. Probably too cold for him. He's a right chancer, must be the ace chancer of all time, a very smart wee bloke. It's amazing to think how many wee gods we have wandering about the place now.

Scotland breeds a different kind of person, and that makes it very hard for people like the wee fat Guru to catch on up here. I think John Knox was the last straw for most people in Scotland. And Calvin, the cold wind from Geneva. So I think by now we've all had our bellyful and we can't really cope with any more.

Guilt is another thing the Church has a lot to answer for.
'Your willy is Dirty. Nasty. Bad.' They think you should cut
them off or something. I worked beside a Jehovah's
Witness at the yards and he used to take his out with a
hankie when he was having a pee. And look the other way!

No, the Scottish people don't tolerate those instant gods very
easily. There was once a cult here called the Nameless
Ones and I think they got about four members.

Mind you, the North of Scotland is quite different. I don't
think you could spring anything new on them at all. The
Closed Brethren would take a bit of beating, I would think.

I believe in all that stuff about the planets and the moon.
Why not? More than I believe in God, I suppose . . . or if
God does exist, he's certainly nothing to do with the Pope
and all that fancy dressing up and paintings on the walls
and all the number that the Bishops get into. The Apaches
didn't have gods at all, and they had a pretty good idea of
what was happening.

But I don't like all the rubbish you get from people
about the stars, all the 'What's-your-sign-man?' stuff. I'm
a Sagittarius, which is quite a good one to be – it means
you've got a licence to shit in the street, because you're half
a horse.

Gerry Rafferty and I were once down in London, playing
at the Roundhouse when this hippie woman came up to
him:

'Hey, man, what . . . like . . . er . . . what sign are you, man?'

'Oh, I used to be Capricorn but I had it changed by deed poll and now I'm a Taurus.'

'What was that, man?' she goes, in this very stoned way. 'What was that you were saying, man?'

'Oh, yes, in Scotland you can just go along to the Registry Office and have it changed.'

'Wow, that's far out, man. I never ... er ... heard of that before ... wow ...'

But sometimes I'll hear the bells ringing in Glasgow at six o'clock on a Sunday evening and I'll think, Oh, I must pop along to Evensong. They have such lovely, lovely hymns ... like 'Up your bum with a broken bottle' ... that's a lovely one, beautiful words.

MATERIAL, INSPIRATIONS, SOURCES & VINEGAR How Adolf Hitler died in Aberdeen

There are some areas that I have never dealt with on stage and never done any patter on, but I don't think there is any subject I would *never* deal in at all.

Sex, for instance, I have never done very much on, because I think I would have to come at it from a very different angle. I don't like those sort of honeymoon jokes or the ones about guys finding their wives in bed with someone.

But there's always the exception, isn't there? Like the one about the Glasgow wedding:

There's this big reception in somebody's house after the wedding and everyone's having a great time, getting tore into the bevvy, dancing and lots of music, HULLLOOOOO, and leaping around, everyone getting blootered. Then suddenly someone rushes into the room where the party's going on and shouts:

'The party's over! On your bikes! SOMEBODY'S FUCKED THE BRIDE!'

That's it. Everyone starts to get their coats on, the music stops, they're all about to go. Then the same guy comes running back into the room:

'It's all right! Dinnae go away! HE'S APOLOGIZED!'

But I've never really thought out how I could do something really funny on sex. And I certainly don't want to sound like Bernard Manning and that sort of comedian.

The way I thought of bringing it in is the way I introduce a lot of my material: how I came across it in the first place; how I found it and it found me.

So I would do wee approaches on the Durex thing – going into a chemist when I was twelve, with a bonnet on and a pipe and a gruff voice. Ending up with aspirins because you get served by a woman. That sort of thing.

And I would bring in all that stuff about carrying Durex around in your pocket when you're at school. You never use the things, of course, but you carry them around with you all the time . . . pulling them out of your pocket and counting them:

'Jesus – have I only got two left?'

– right in front of your pals. And I would like to get into why it is that barbers sell Durex. Why them, in the name of God?

Why do barbers sell Durex?
That's what we all want to know . . .

It blew my mind in Dublin that no-one there can have contraceptives. That's bloody crazy, isn't it? I was thinking of taking some in with me when we went and blowing them up . . . 'They're for the wain's party – honest.'

My cousin, who lives in Ireland, in a place called Ness, I think, got this parcel once from England. And it was at the time of all the letter bombs and things and it looked quite suspicious. So he got the police in and they've got these really sophisticated explosive things now, so that they can blow open a letter with just a tiny charge and it hardly damages the contents. So they took the package outside, put a wee explosive in it and BOOM. But it wasn't quite enough, didn't get the package open and they can just see this tin thing which gives their equipment a reaction. So they reckon it must be something in it, get everyone to stand back and put in a bigger explosive. BOOOOOM. And a great shower of Durex goes floating into everyone's gardens! The tin foil they're wrapped in must have activated it and there's all the neighbours rushing around gathering them up. It's raining Durex in Ireland . . .

One guy I knew – and this is a lie – had this nervous tic that would make him look as though he was winking at you all the time. And I was asking him if there wasn't something he could do about it, if there wasn't something he could take to make it better . . .

'Aye, Billy (wink) . . . I take aspirin for it. It (wink) makes it a wee bit better. I suppose (wink) I should take one now.'

So he reaches into his pockets and brings out packet after packet of Durex, piling them up on the table.

'What have ye got a' that Durex for, for Chrissake?'

'Well, every time I go intae the chemist (wink) and I ask the man behind the counter (wink) for some aspirin . . .'

In the meantime, I steer clear of all that innuendo rubbish, all the sniggery type of jokes that they do on TV . . . But I have a wee routine with Billy Johnstone about sexual perversions . . . You know, the woman is coming back late at night to the house of some punter she's never met before that evening and he starts heating the poker in the fire: 'I hope you'll learn to understand my little eccentricities . . .'

The really pornographic stuff I just find pretty boring. I remember watching blue movies after a gig in Edinburgh and we ran the film backwards – couples with no clothes on suddenly getting dressed, starting to have a cup of tea, the bodies all springing away from each other. That was great. But the rest of them are pretty bloody tedious.

I would only put in jokes about homosexuals if they were in context. The willy-watcher, for instance, the guy who looks at your willy in the public toilet, is really a very sad figure. But I'm not saying anything about *him* when I do that piece in my act about willy-watching; it's *my* reaction to him that I'm talking about and that's quite clear and quite a different thing.

I'm not a minority-basher and I never will be. But I must say that your first encounter with a guy like the willy-watcher can be very distressing and therefore can be funny. So I make it funny.

Drugs is something I've not done much on in my acts. I do make that joke about Mandrax the Magician, but there's an awful lot of guys doing that sort of thing and they're obviously a lot . . . wiser on the drug scene than I am. Richard Pryor and people like that do routines on snorting coke, but I've just got very, very little experience. I don't want to close doors on those sorts of things, I just want to wait for an opportunity to come along so that if I have an idea I can get it all in context.

So I steer clear of jokes about limp wrists and homosexuality, where it's so easy to get a quick snigger. And all these Irish jokes get a bit tedious, although there is the odd funny one that makes me laugh, like the Irish Evel Knievel – drives a London bus over thirteen motorcycles.

And I do love doing parody stuff. When I saw Tammy Wynette at the Apollo, I couldn't believe it – I must have got a year's worth of material out of that. She was singing these really sad songs and I would be rolling about on the floor, biting the carpet. I love that whole kind of 'Country and Western' sincere bit:

'Well, ah – it's ah really great to be back in – (where the hell are we, boys?) – ah, yes, back in Glasgow . . . We really love ya – don't we, boys?'

And then they'll play these cowboy songs: 'I've been so Lonesome in the Saddle since my horse died.' I used to picture this guy riding through the desert on a roller skate. Anyway, I get a lot of material from those guys:

Please don't spew on my pillow,
Push your warm and sweaty semmit close to mine . . .

and:

I've got piles,
You've got scabies,
The wain's got the measles
And the dog's got the rabies,
Oh Boy . . .

I'm losin' ma hair,
Ma arches are fallin',
Our six wains
Are always bawlin'.

There's nappies in the kitchen,
Toys on the stairs,
When I ask you for support, you shout
'Up the Gers . . .'

All my life,
I've been kissin'
Your left tit,
'Cause the right one's missin',
Oh, Boy . . .

It's interesting to see the reactions of different audiences in different parts of the country to the jokes and stuff that I do. Sometimes I do a piece that I think is hilarious and – nothing.

In Aberdeen, I told this joke about Hitler:

There are these guys whose plane crashes in the middle of the jungle in Brazil and they stagger out and beat their way through the undergrowth until, after many days of travelling, they come to this clearing. And there they see this wee bloke with hair brushed across and the little moustache.

'Eh, excuse me, pal, hope ye dinnae mind me askin' – but are you no' Adolf Hitler?'

'Aye. What aboot it?'

'Well what are ye doin' oot here in the jungle an' that?'

Hitler looks up from all these books and maps and papers that he's been studying.

'I'm plannin' the Fourth Reich . . . And this time I'm no' goin' tae make any mistakes. This time it's goin' tae be: NO MORE MISTER NICE GUY!'

Died on its arse, that did. So I dropped it.

Then there's the wee bit about Mary Whitehouse in the middle of the patter about Kenneth Tynan saying Fuck on TV:

'Mrs Whitehouse lost the place completely. Mind you, I wouldnae be very happy if my name rhymed wi' toilet.'

Some people get it right away. The others are all going 'Whitehouse–Lavvie . . . doesnae work . . .'

The problem with comedy stuff is that it dies so quickly, particularly if you put it on an album. It's all right for those rock and roll stars, they've got it made. They all go into the studio together and rehearse, do twelve tracks, no bother. But my material has to mature and get ready and whenever it's ready and on record – boof, it's dead.

There are two guys in Scotland, comedians, who will actually record a comedy album and then go out and perform it as well. It's not quite the funniest thing you ever saw.

But there are all sorts of comedians that I like and admire. I liked the Monty Python stuff and Frankie Howerd and Chic Murray, although I wish he would do on stage what he does off stage because when he's doing his patter at a party or something, he's really magic.

Jack Radcliffe was one of my favourite comedians. He used to do a brilliant imitation of a Glasgow drunk. And if you talked to people who had seen it, afterwards, they would always think that he had been staggering around all over the stage, whereas in fact he had been standing on the one spot – walking on the one leg.

And Tony Hancock was great, although sometimes I thought he went over the top a bit with over-acting, the way the English actors do. But I loved his Blood Donor piece, particularly because when I was in the yards, I used to give blood at the Southern General Hospital. I felt like a hero. My blood wasn't one of the rare ones, but when there was an accident I would always be called on one of the first because my name was Connolly and I was near the beginning of the alphabet. So off I would go and have the afternoon off work.

I've always read a lot. When I was working at the bookshop, I read just about everything that Nevil Shute ever wrote, although I find him a very childish writer now. I always liked P. G. Wodehouse and I've read just about everything he wrote. Orwell I liked a lot and I kind of sickened myself with a great glut of him – *The Road to Wigan Pier* was my favourite. I loved it.

After that, it was anybody. Hemingway and Steinbeck. Anybody worth his salt read Steinbeck and my favourite was *Of Mice and Men*, and another called *Pastures of Heaven* about a wee valley in California, called Pasturas de Cielo and the wee family that used to live there. It was a

Steinbecky Peyton Place, although it wasn't sick like that, but it was taking every character in town and then analysing them. But the first book I read right through was *Lord of the Flies*.

George Bernard Shaw, too. I like some of the things he used to say. One particularly because of what I'm doing now – he sent a card to Churchill inviting him to the first night of his play and he put: 'Bring a friend – if you have one.' Churchill writes back and says he can't make the first night, but he'll come to the second night, ' – if you have one.'

I read vast amounts of non-fiction when I was at school. I really liked Tibet and read everything I could about it . . . I have that Tibetan guy on the side of Loch Lomond in the introduction to the Welly Boot song now. I always wanted very badly to go to Tibet and felt really cheated when the Chinese did a number on it. Not that the Chinese were right or wrong or whatever, just that they closed the door for me as it were; I'd never ever see it.

The whole Tibetan number used to fascinate me: washing in butter, kite-flying, prayer wheels, the whole trip. I read *Seven Years in Tibet* and after that I went through anything I could lay my hands on.

Then I went into a Japan trip and read everything on that, because I found it a really interesting place. And I tried to read about China, but it was virtually impossible. I even bought Mao's life story, the paperback, and it was hellish. By the third page, you've forgotten who everybody is. You know . . . was that Lin See Piao or was it Sin Lee Piao? Impossible, quite impossible. Two thirds of the book was index.

I like Solzhenitsyn, too, and my favourite of his was *A Day in the Life of Ivan Denisovitch*. And I got stuck into *The First Circle* and *Cancer Ward*, too.

We had to read Sir Walter Scott at school – *Ivanhoe*. I hated them all. And R. L. Stevenson, too. Hated him. And then I was doing my Oxfam number, buying a yard of books at a sale, which Iris usually does, and one of them was *Dr Jekyll and Mr Hyde* and I read it again and it was outstandingly good. I'll never part with it, because I love the language so much ... 'I repaired immediately to my apartment ...'

But I didn't like Scott at all. Hated *Black Arrow* and *Heart of Midlothian*. And I hated what they did to Shakespeare at school, too. 'Learn that passage,' and all that nonsense. It's OK for an actor to learn that passage if he has to go and bloody perform it, but why the hell did we have to? It should be read like a book.

It's legendary what they do to poetry at schools, too. Wordsworth, Burns ... Burns I hated at school. Not because of anything in his writing, but because of the kind of guys who were good at it. They were always the kind of guys I hated, and they would win the Burns prize. I hated the way they would read the stuff out, real pretentious little mammie's boys they were.

As regards Scottish writers ... I read *No Mean City* and didn't like it at all. I like Archie Hynds's stuff, the guy who wrote *The Dear Green Place*; he's got an odd job now – resident writer in Aberdeen; I don't think very much of that idea, though I like Archie personally. And Alan Sharp's stuff appeals to me. I've read a few of Gordon Williams's – that book of his, *Walk, Don't Walk*, I just couldn't believe when I read it.

Some of the poets I like, too. Tom Leonard and Tom Buchan. And Hamish Henderson of the School of Scottish Studies is one of my favourite people. I love the pieces he does for magazines, that incredible insight he has, whether he's talking about folk music or folk culture or whatever.

A Drunk Man Looks at The Thistle by Hugh Macdiarmaid was something else I loved. But then everybody knows he's a genius, so it's silly for me to even try and explain why I like him. Someone told me that he liked my stuff and it blew my head off, I couldn't believe it. I like being respected by people I respect.

When I was on the road with the Humblebums, doing a lot of one-nighters, I would buy a vast cross-section of stuff to read in railway stations. And my prayers were finally answered when *Rolling Stone* came out. That gave me hours and hours of pleasure. Up until then I had only *Melody Maker* and *Sounds* which were expressing any kind of opinion the same as mine . . . when I was living down in London, I always used to nip down to Tottenham Court Road to get the latest copy of *Melody Maker* and it always pissed me off that they would list us under the Folk section.

I didn't like *IT* and *Oz*, they were too much of a wank for me; the writers thought they were the only ones who knew. But I like *National Lampoon*, I like the freedom that that represents – or represented perhaps. *Private Eye* I eventually liked, though not at first. I thought it was a wee bit highbrow for me, college-boy funny. But sometimes the guys were so subtle in their writing that I would think they were being serious when they were actually taking the piss. And I would say Fascist Bastards! and throw it down . . . and in actual fact the guy was getting the boot in.

As for newspapers, I still read the *Daily Record* and the *Sunday Post*, because I get so many ideas from them. I used to read the *Evening News* in London, because of the wee short story that I could sit reading on the tube. At that time I got into the *Observer* and I remember thinking the first time that I bought it, that I was a real pseud. I was saying to myself:

'What the hell are you buying these for – you'll never understand them.' But the *Observer* Review was a smashing wee paper and Hugh McIlvanney takes some beating . . . McIlviolence . . . McIlvino . . .

But I love words, love coming across new ones. And it saddens me when you run into censorship, because people don't like you to use certain words that everyone uses every day anyway.

Like they wouldn't plug my record 'D-I-V-O-R-C-E' on the radio in Dublin, because I used the word 'bum'. And they've had to put bleeps on it so that they can put it on the BBC. They wouldn't let me say 'F-ing C'. But when I was on the Parkinson show, I asked him if it was OK to sing it and he said 'Sure, you've already censored it yourself by saying "F-ing C". Go right ahead.' But the BBC are funny about things like that. They let Little Richard sing about 'balling'; but I suppose that was because they didn't know what it meant – they thought he was singing 'bawling'.

Remember Lenny Bruce? He was on stage once, in San Francisco, I think it was, and there are all these policemen in the audience waiting to bust him for using obscene language. So he gets up on the stage and explains to the audience that because of the police being there, he's going to use different words. Like when he wants to say a four-letter word that starts in C and ends in T, he'll say 'tulip'. And when he's going to say a word that starts in F and ends in K, he'll say 'daffodil'. And the word that starts in B and ends in D will be 'rhododendron'. Right? He checks up that everyone has got it – 'tulip', 'daffodil', 'rhododendron'. Then he starts off:

'Well, there was this Mexican cocksucker . . .'

I don't have to explain many of the words I use in the show to English audiences. There are a few that I translate, like 'chanty', a chamberpot and 'semmit' a vest. Or a word like 'glaikit', which everyone in Scotland knows, but I would explain that a 'glaikit' person is someone who, when he comes into a room, you get a feeling that someone just walked out.

I remember when I first came down to London, going into one of the wee off-licence places to get a carry-out – we were off to some party or something. I was ordering up the cans of Export and the half-bottle and getting them all on the counter. He's just looking at me, waiting for me to pick them all up:

'Where's the carry-oot bag?'
'What?'
'A *carry-oot* . . .'

The guy didn't have a clue what I was talking about at all. And he's looking at me and going: 'Oh, maybe I have a box you could put them in . . .'

I love coming across new words. Like in those Sci Fi books about weird things, – not about space, which I tend to find pretty boring – but about all the odd stuff. They often have very strange words, like 'cusp'. That's a lovely word.

My favourite word is 'hideous'. I don't know why, but I just think it's a smashing word. I notice new words when I read them or hear them and I tuck them away, not consciously, but it works itself in somehow. I've been in the business nine years now, so tucking away words is a natural process and they tend to come out at random. They even come out at the wrong time sometimes.

I got one from Burroughs' *Naked Lunch*, which I like very much: 'amorphosize' . . . And there are other words I like to use: 'molecate' is very descriptive. It's just a childhood word, means to give someone a doing. I've no idea what it comes from.

And I found this expression in *In Cold Blood* by Truman Capote . . . 'There'll be blood and hair on the walls.' That says a lot, doesn't it . . . 'Blood and hair on the walls.'

But when it comes right down to it, I still get most of my stuff from punters in the pubs. Like I was having a pint in the Horseshoe Bar at lunchtime and a guy told me about John Wayne:

He's drinking in this saloon bar, having six whiskies, knocks them back one after the other and then goes out to get his horse and ride off. Someone's taken it. So Big John looks round all the people in the street and says:

'OK. I'm going back inside the saloon and I'm going to have one more whisky. And when I come out again, I want to see that horse back there waiting for me. Or else the same thing that happened in Denver when they took my horse is going to happen right here.'

So he goes back inside the saloon, has his whisky and strides out again. There's his horse, all neatly tethered to the rail. Hops on to it and starts to ride out of town. And one of the local guys comes up to him and says:

'Hey, John . . . what *did* happen in Denver?'
'I had to fuckin' walk home.'

FAME, FORTUNE & FUTURE
Marx & Lenin in Paris, a Stoatter in Dundee & Sedan Chairs in Drymen

I was talking about being famous to some other 'stars' and they were all saying that it's not you that changes, it's the people around you.

My dad can't go into his local in Partick any more because the manager keeps pointing him out to people: 'That's Billy Connolly's father, see, over there . . .' And when I go in now, he calls me '*Mr* Connolly'. I mean, I've been drinking in there for twelve years and suddenly I'm *Mr* Connolly.

I get people coming up to me a lot, too, asking: 'How come you're a Socialist and you've got that big hoose and that big car and a' that money, eh?'

But that's their idea of socialism, not mine. *I* never said that I thought everyone should be poor. But the Tories like to paint this picture of socialism as meaning that everyone gets worse off, instead of better off.

I tell them that story about Karl Marx arriving in Paris. Lenin is there to meet him at the station and as the train comes in, Lenin sees that Marx is in a First Class compartment. Lenin's amazed, really shocked. So Marx says to him:

'Ye've got it a' wrang. Everyone thinks that when the revolution comes, we'll get rid of all the First Class stuff. But that's what we'll *keep*. The rubbish we'll get rid of.'

I get shouted at a lot in the street now. Most of it's friendly:
'See you, Big Yin!' But you get people going: 'HEY – you—
you're *rubbish*!' But that's fair enough. I do a lot of shouting
myself.

Some of the women that come up to me are downright cheeky:

'I don't like you personally, but could you sign this for my
friend?'

Which is not the nicest possible thing in the world to say to
someone. But there you go; so many of the others are so
nice that it balances out.

It's funny, too, that people always go on about groupies:
'Eh, d'ye get . . . eh . . . lots of lumber . . . aye, ye must have
a' thae women comin' roond, an' that . . . eh?' But I get
many more *blokes* coming round for autographs and hanging
outside the dressing-room or the stage door. There were
two wee lassies in Aberdeen who came every night and
waited outside in the rain and kept phoning up the office.
But I don't like that kind of thing very much.

A drunk guy came up to me in Dumfries once, going into
these furious outbursts. I was with Ronnie Carroll, who's
a very, very nice man, and we were sitting together in the
hotel lounge, and the guy recognized us both. He kept
trying to get into the conversation, making wee remarks,
and nobody wanted to know – he was a real loud-mouthed
bore. Eventually he jumps up and says to me:

'YOU – it's a long way doon! Always remember that. Aye,
you're at the top just now but you'll come doon. And
YOU,' he says to Ronnie Carroll, 'you're a *has-been* . . .
I played for *Scotland*.'

I just burst out laughing, I couldn't take it at all. Then he came up with the never-to-be-forgotten line.

'I FOUGHT FOR YOU!'

He'd fought in the war and played for Scotland and he thought, Talk to Me. It was terrible. And it was made even more terrible by the fact that the manager of the hotel had pulled his wife, so he couldn't leave after he'd made his outburst, because he couldn't find her. Oh, it was sad.

Ronnie Carroll is a very funny man. He told us he'd been staying in this hotel and having a meal there; and he's on a special diet. So he calls over the waitress:

'I'd like a steak, grilled not fried. No potatoes. And some carrots and asparagus tips.'

Off she goes and comes back twenty minutes later with his dinner. There's the steak, sure enough, and the carrots, but no asparagus tips.

'Er . . . where's the asparagus tips?'

'Oh, I'm very sorry – we've only got Benson and Hedges.'

He was performing in one place where the people were really rude, talking all the way through the show, the cashier's ringing up the change on the cash register while he's trying to sing, chaos. Anyway, at the end of the show, the manager of the club comes up to him.

'Er . . . didn't go down too well tonight, did it?'

'Never mind,' says Ronnie. 'I think it went over the top of their heads.'

So next night he's back there before the show starts and the manager comes up to him, beaming away.

'It's going to be fine tonight, Ronnie – I've lowered the speakers by two feet . . .'

I don't really mind all that stuff you get on the street in Glasgow, the 'HULLLOOO, BIG YIN!' number and everything. But I think sometimes that the Glasgow audiences know me so well now that they come along to the shows in a very critical way. You know, they're going on to the person sitting beside them:

'Oh, he's got much better stuff than this . . . the last time I saw him he had this *really* funny joke . . . oh, aye, you should have seen him when blahbetty blah . . .'

But I suppose that's bound to happen. Like the stuff I get from the folkies who think I've sold out, all the 'Come back home, Billy, we still love you' rubbish that they keep giving you.

What the folkies think about me having a great big orchestra behind me is not a matter of the greatest importance to me. As far as they're concerned, you can have *fiddles* playing with you, but not *violins*. I do a show to please myself, not to please the folkies. And if they think that having strings and brass is schmaltzy, I don't care. If I want a big bloody orchestra, I'll have one.

They had a go at me in Sandy Bell's *Broadsheet*, and *Edinburgh Folk* magazine. They're just like the Dundee papers . . . and they spelled the word 'shite' with an asterisk instead of an 'i' – so that tells you where they're coming from.

The other thing I get a lot of is people coming up to me and saying:

'It's awright for you. You just have tae get up on the stage and tell jokes . . . Aye, you've had a really lucky break.'

And it reminds me of the story about Arnold Palmer, the golfer. He was playing in this big golf tournament somewhere and he hits the ball on to the top of the bunker and it sticks there – thunk! So he takes out a club and does this delicate wee chip. The ball goes right up, out of the bunker and lands just beside the hole, a few inches away. One of the spectators comes up to Palmer.

'You were lucky there, Arnold.'

'Yes,' he says. 'And it's an amazing thing: but the more I practise, the luckier I get.'

I wish I'd said that.

I get a lot of letters all the time and I used to read them all myself. I even get ones that are just addressed to 'The Big Yin, Scotland' and come all the way from Canada. But now the office deal with them. I sign all the photos, there's no rubber stamp or any of that.

And you get asked to personalize them, too. 'To Granny for her birthday' and 'To Jeannie'. That way I have a fair idea of the sort of names that are popular at the moment. There's a lot of Jonathans for some reason and a lot of Karens.

There are plenty of abusive ones, too. One guy wrote to me and said:

'I've seen all the comedians come and go since the early thirties. And I can tell you that you are by far the worst. If you're a comedian, I'm a Chinaman.'

And he put his name and address at the bottom, which a lot of them don't. So I wrote to him:

'I'm sorry if you've got that opinion, because in my opinion I'm the best.'

I got it back 'Not Known at this Address'. He hadn't even got the courage to put his real name down.

In Dundee, I got this hate letter delivered to the dressing-room, written on top of the advertisement for the show. It was a real stoatter.

'You make more money than top surgeons. You make your money out of getting dirty laughs. What sort of an example do you think you're setting for young girls and chaps like us. Go back to Ireland. The Army needs you there. You never did an honest day's work in your life.' Aye, that was anonymous too.

I get sent a lot of scripts, too. Most of them are dreadful. Usually they're weak imitations of what I do at the moment. And they try and write them in that phonetic Glasgow way and always get it completely wrong. They always try and countrify it and put in words like 'ken' ... 'D'ye ken the noo' ... It's very odd.

But it must be very difficult for any professional comedian to write anything for me. I'm sorry about that in some ways because it would be very convenient. But, in the end, I think it's probably better that way. I'm popular enough now to decide when to go on tour; I don't *have* to work for money any more, so I can wait until I've got something that I think is right for a show and then do it.

I don't mind the signing autographs number, but people come up to you at the worst possible times. Like you're just about to go on stage in two minutes and someone will sneak through and say: 'Sign that, will you? And put "To Alec with Best Wishes" on it.' And there I am in my tights or something ready to do the show and all nervous and up for it. But they don't realize that. And if I refuse to sign, they get all sarcastic and unpleasant about it.

The old ladies are the worst. They see you in a crowd and want to get an autograph, but they can't push their way right to the front, so they grab hold of a piece of you. And you get carried away by the crowd but the old lady is still hanging on to your velvet jacket – she can't see you any more because of all the people, but she's determined not to let go.

The people who work at the halls are always coming up to you, too: 'Could you sign this for an old lady – she's in a geriatric hospital and she's your greatest fan . . . Sign this one in braille . . . ' Just when you're about to leap on stage and start your act. Oh, it's murder-polis all right.

There was a young bloke came up to me to get an autograph when I was on stage in Preston, just before the end of the show, but I still had two songs to go. So I signed his programme. I just thought what it would have been like for him having to go back to his mates without it, having done all the number of coming to the stage in front of everyone. So I figured that there wasn't going to be a rush; he was the only one there, so I could do it. And there was no way I could have gone on and sung the songs with his wee face peering up at me – it's like when you're in a pub trying to talk to your mates and there's a television there which you just can't take your eyes off.

A tattooed guy got me to sign on his arm so that he could have the autograph tattooed on. His whole arm was covered in tattoos, so he found this one wee piece of pink flesh and I signed there and he said he was off to get it tattooed that night. But I'm not too keen on signing on people's bodies.

One wee fly-man nearly got me to sign an agreement for something – ordering curtains or blinds or something. He just thrust the piece of paper at me when there was a whole crowd trying to get autographs and I went: 'Wait a minute . . .'

Another time, I was at the Celtic–Dundee Cup Final at Hampden Park, sitting watching the game. This wee guy starts working his way up from the front to where I'm sitting, climbs his way along the row, clambering over people, and finally gets to me:

'Hey, Big Yin – sign this, will you?'
'Oh, I'm watching the game.'
'*Please*, Big Yin . . .'
'Oh, all right . . . what d'you want me to write?'
'Just write: "Jean, you're a shitehouse", and sign it' . . .

I only ever got two autographs myself. One was Alex Campbell and the other was Tom Paxton. Then, years later, I was on the same bill as him, which really delighted me.

But I wasn't a very autography kind of person; there were very few around when I was a boy. It was considered a bit English, like train-spotting. I've yet to see a Scottish train-spotter . . . can you imagine a West Highlands train-spotter? One number in his book? It seems like an exclusively English hobby, like catching butterflies. Mind you, if you could *eat* butterflies, Scotsmen would be the best people in the world at catching them.

One thing I don't like about the whole show business thing is the amount of slagging off that goes on. I don't like people attacking the Bay City Rollers all the time, for instance. Everyone gets very superior about them all the time. Why can they not leave them alone? If they've not got anything, they'll disappear in a wee while anyway.

There's so much jealousy in the business, so much needle. When the Beatles started off, after all, they were pretty rough. Let's face it, that Shea Stadium gig they did was pretty raw. And some of their early songs were awful. No, the Rollers are all right. They don't do any harm.

Another thing I don't like is that big number they've been doing on dead stars recently. James Dean and Marilyn Monroe. I thought James Dean was a right phoney. And Marilyn Monroe . . . I'd rather have Beryl Reid. I think she's a great actress, much better than Marilyn Monroe.

But I do like the whole 'star' thing. I've always been into it, the whole *A Star is Born* kind of number. Which is why I've been paying taxes and getting all that kind of rubbish out of the way, because I don't want *anything* to interfere with it. I know guys that can't appear on television because they don't want the Inland Revenue to find out what they're doing. I don't want any of that kind of bother.

And I enjoy doing the sort of things you get asked to do, like handing out the prizes at the *Melody Maker* awards in London. It was strange seeing all these faces there. Bob Harris . . . the man with the Iron Moustache. John Peel . . . the great-grandson of the founder of our police force.

I like being able to meet people I've always wanted to meet. Like Jimmy Shand, the dance-band bloke, what a nice wee man. And he's a motorcycle freak, are you ready for that? Lives in Fife and drives around on this great big bike. We saw him having breakfast at the Peebles Hydro, just sitting on his own. And he orders toast and honey with a cup of tea. The waitress gave him one of those wee individual pots of honey and he says to her:

'I see you keep a bee . . .'

Jean Marsh, from *Upstairs Downstairs*, I've always admired, so it was nice to meet her. I told her I'd always liked what she did, and she said:

'That's not you that keeps sending me those letters saying how you'd like to do it with me – but only if I'm still wearing the uniform?'

'Naw . . . I'm the breather.'

I have a strange relationship with the press. For instance, in Scotland on my last tour, a lot of the Scottish press thought that I was very offensive because I talked about willies and jobbies and farting and snotters. And a lot of them like to see me as a sort of couthy Mr Glasgow, but no way am I that.

Journalists, a lot of them, I think, are parasites.

There was one time I was at a party in Parkhead and this journalist sneaked in without being invited and we eventually found him making notes in the lavvie! He'd been listening all the time, then scribbling it down, overhearing stuff and rushing off to where no one could see him, to scribble. The next day we were to have had a press conference, but he blew the whole thing because he had the story first. So only two guys showed up at the conference.

But it was dumb on the part of that journalist, because no way will I ever do anything for him again, no way. It's different behaving like that if you're exposing something important, like Watergate. But that kind of parasitical, sneaky journalism I hate. Then they go on and talk about the Freedom of the Press – but most of the papers are owned by the Tories anyway. So where's the freedom there?

The *Scottish Daily News* got tore into me for a while. When they started off, they put me down for a £5,000 contribution and do you know the name of the guy they sent round to try and get money from me? CADGER! A guy called Bill Cadger came round – can you get the mentality of that? There's probably five of them on the committee and they have to choose the guy called Cadger to send off to hustle the money.

I get fed up with being compared to Lenny Bruce all the time. I don't think I'm anything like him at all, although I love some of the things he did and said. Perhaps I resemble some of the American comics who were influenced by him, but until all the papers and interviews started doing this comparison, I had never even heard what the guy sounded like. I knew who he was, but I didn't know what his patter was like, so I went out and bought a stack of his records.

All people in show business are fed up with being compared to people in the press, being told they're like So-and-So, or 'Scotland's answer to So-and-So'. But I never based my act on anyone. It just grew, in an organic fashion, just grew by itself, leading me along by the tongue. Yet people go on comparing me to Lenny Bruce.

Still, there are worse people I could be compared to – it could be Bernard Manning. He's been making cracks about me to start up some action for himself, I suppose. The American comics used to do that number – Bob Hope would make cracks about Bing Crosby or Jack Benny.

I've always had a hard time with D. C. Thomson, who publish the *Sunday Post* and all the Dundee papers. They interviewed me for The Honest Truth, their personality column, and at that time they weren't employing anyone who belonged to a union. When they asked me what I would like to be if I wasn't in show business, I told them I'd like to be a full-time trades union organizer. They never printed it. They might as well have run the story, 'CONNOLLY RECORDS SELL WELL IN RUSSIA!'

Dundee used to be known for its jute, jam and journalism. I hope it's still all right for jute and jam.

But I still get the *Sunday Post* because it gives me so many ideas. One of the favourite things I saw in it was:

'Can you please settle a family argument – how tall is Kenneth McKellar?'

Can you picture the family all arguing away . . . 'Naw, it's five foot seven . . . Naw, it isnae . . . it's at least five foot nine . . . Rubbish, it's . . .'

'Dear Doctor', which is their medical column, really cracks me up, too.

'Dear Doctor, I have a large red lump on my leg, which bleeds all night . . .'

Can you imagine sitting down and writing a letter like that? I'd be away down to the doctor in case it ate my leg off . . .

'Dear Doctor, My leg has turned black and dropped off . . .' They're quite amazing some of them.

And Nature Man, who's always doing wee articles under titles like 'Murder in the Glen'. 'Murder in the Glen' – just because some ferret got tore into some other wee animal:

'The mighty golden eagle stalked its prey, the small grey ferret, as it darted through the heather . . . it circled, hovered, then pounced. In a trice, the ferret was ensconced in the eagle's claw . . . This would have ended in bloody murder had it not been for two holiday-makers from Govan, who chanced by and battered the eagle to death with an empty Irn Bru bottle . . .'

Hon Man is another who always gives me a laugh. The HON stands for Holidays On Nothing. He used to try and get from Glasgow to Paris on fourpence.

The *Sunday Post* is ducks-on-the-wall stuff for a Scottish home, no house would be complete without it. It wasn't until someone told me what a dreadful paper it was that I realized I never read it. I really had to *look* for the bad bits. It has saturation coverage in Scotland, but no one actually reads it. They just flick through it; no one really takes in all that anti-union stuff they have in the paper, or the leader columns – only the people who have a direct interest in politics or something. But very, very few people read things like 'As We See It' and 'Have You Heard?'.

Another thing that D. C. Thomson's do and I get a lot of laughs from are their Love Stories . . .

'Janet's bright smile merely masked the deep sadness and loneliness in her heart. Alec had been dead for nearly a year now and it was a struggle bringing up the twins on her own . . . When she met Douglas who ran the bakery at the bottom of the street, she suddenly found herself feeling nervous, girlish even . . . "Will you be our new daddy?" the twins asked him, when he brought them home from a day in the country. He smiled at them with his dark-brown eyes and Janet could see the corner of his mouth turn up under his thick, black moustache. "Not fucking likely," he said as he rolled himself another thick joint . . .'

I have to get away from all the madness and the press and everything now, though. Not all the time, because I get itchy to go on tour or just do a wee show or something. But I took up fishing recently to get away from things a bit.

Fly-fishing is what I would like to be really good at. One guy I know can cast his line the length of a football park. And learning the whole art of it really appeals to me. Not that catching fish has got much to do with it anyway. If you catch one, all the better; if you don't it doesn't matter. Anyway, the woman in the pub catches more fish in her nightie than I do with the rod . . .

The first time I was taken fishing, I was very fortunate because I went with a pal of mine, Ronnie Montgomery, who not only knows a lot about fishing, but he can tell you about the birds, what they're doing, about the plants, and what kind of grubs you get under what kind of plants and what's good for bait. And suddenly the whole scenario opens up to you and it's so totally divorced from what I do the rest of the time that it's really refreshing. It really wakens me up, gets that sort of jaded curtain that comes over you out of the way. A real spiritual uplift.

When I went to Barbados with Iris and the kids – aye, you should have seen my Barbados tan – I did a lot of snorkelling. And a wee bit of the back-of-the-boat deep-sea fishing, all strapped in. Caught a beauty, a fifty-pound

kingfish. But when I was snorkelling, I just looked at the
fish and they came up and looked at me. It was incredible
the way they come at you, like rain on the windscreen.
Me in the middle and all these great wee fish coming at me.

Knowing so little about fish, I was hoping they're not
piranha, hoping my arse would still be there when I turned
round – all that's left is a false tooth and a snorkel.

People get piranhas as pets and feed them wee animals.
Drop a mouse in and watch the piranhas tearing great
lumps off it – that's not fair. The same guys usually have
swords and guns on their wall. And they learn karate –
hoping to get attacked. Every night they go to bed, hoping
that someone's going to leap on them so that they can give
them a 'gashi-kashi'.

But those guys who collect knives and guns, I've always
treated with respect. I avoid them like the plague. And the
people who collect Nazi souvenirs, there's something very,
very odd about that.

All I have in the way of guns is a ·22 air-rifle. But I've just
had an offer to do some clay-pigeon shooting. So I'll try
that and if I like it, I'll buy a gun. It's a thing that's always
attracted me. I like target shooting, too, and when I was in
the Terris, I was quite a good shot. But I don't want to
shoot live things, just clay pigeons. Except, instead of clay
pigeons, I'll use Bill Barclay albums. Or Bernard Manning's
new single.

A couple of years ago, I used to think that if I really made some best-selling albums, I could retire if I wanted to. And that sort of appealed to me, retiring before I was forty and doing all those weird and wonderful things and going to all sorts of different places. But now that it's more or less happened, I find that if I'm not working, I get unsettled and want to work again. Not that I don't like being out in the country, in Drymen. It's so bloody beautiful out there and so quiet – the only noise you hear is the occasional sedan chair going past.

But I would like my career to go more along acting lines now. I'd like to do films more but they take such a long time to happen, you never know whether they're coming off or not. I thoroughly enjoyed doing *Just Another Saturday*, which Peter Macdougall wrote, I found that a real pleasure.

The film that I did about the Clyde, *Clydeoscope*, I saw was showing on the same bill as a John Wayne movie, which really cracked me up – me and John Wayne, eh? So I've kept the cutting.

But I don't mind if I end up skint. I've been down that road before and it doesn't bother me. I've no idea how I'll end up . . . but, one thing, I wouldn't ever be cremated . . .

Dominic Behan told me once that he and Brendan were on the ferry over to France, which was a place that Brendan dearly loved, and they found this guy scattering his father's ashes over the edge of the boat, because his dad had asked to be thrown out over the Channel when he died. The ashes were all blowing about all over the place while Dominic and Brendan were trying to eat their sandwiches. So Dominic says:

'Hey, Brendan, – d'ye no' want to finish your ham-and-daddy sandwich?'

A guy at Radio Clyde told me the best epitaph to have. He's going to have the inscription on his gravestone:

'For fuck's sake – is that the time already?'

ODIOUSLY RUDE, OFFENSIVE AND LAVATORIAL STUFF McGlumpher the Lavvie Attendant, Chanty Techniques & If God had meant us to fart he would have given us a funnel
(This chapter should be removed before sending the book to relatives in South Africa.)

I know that some people find my talking about lavvies and jobbies and farting offensive, but there is a reason for it. Because when you're in a public lavvie or a situation like that, you're vulnerable. And when you're vulnerable, you're funny. Anyway . . .

There was a guy in a public toilet, having a piss, and it's spraying about all over the place, like a bloody fountain. And the guys on each side of him are going:

'Ferchrissake! What's happenin'? Look at that – right over ma bloody jecket! That's good mohair, ya tube! Jesus, it's in ma *hair*!'

'I'm very sorry,' says the wee guy, 'I cannae help it . . . it just keeps happenin' . . .'

'Well, you should get somethin' done aboot that, pal. Away and see a doctor!'

So off he goes to see a doctor. Takes his willy out and lays it on the table. The doctor takes out his microscope to examine it.

So he's explaining to the doctor what the trouble is . . .

'It's ma . . . well, I dinnae know the right name fer it . . . I think it's called ma "venus" . . . Every time I go tae the lavvie, it sprays about a' over the place.'

The doctor's looking at it very closely now.

'Good heavens! This is quite amazing. Never in my twenty years of practice have I ever seen anything like it. It's full of holes!'

'Is that right, eh?'

The doctor starts writing out a name on a piece of paper.

'Here. Go and see this man right away.'

'Thanks very much . . . Is he a specialist?'

'No – he's a clarinet player. He'll teach you how to hold it.'

A toilet attendant in Glasgow is retiring after fifty years of service. So the STV cameras are down there to record the event and interviewing him.

'Well, Mr McGlumpher, fifty years service . . . in all that time you must have seen some changes?'

'Have I seen *changes*? I can tell ye: nowadays, there's some punters come in here wi' a bottle o' that cheap wine and go intae the cubicles and drink it. There's others that come in here in twos and go intae the cubicles and I don't know *what* they dae. And there's others come in here and look at each other's willies! I'll tell ye somethin'. When someone comes in here for a shite – it's like a breath of fresh air.'

I talk a lot about chanties. But it occurred to me recently that I'd never actually used one. I used to see lots of them when we went to Rothesay for holidays, in the boarding-houses there. Part of the tea-service it was . . . very handy, too: you could have a cup of cocoa in bed and then just put it underneath.

But there must be a technique to using the chanty. Because you have to do it in the dark. After all, if there's someone else in the room – and if you've any luck at all, there's someone else in the room – you don't want to wake them up by turning on the light: 'Hey, d'ye want tae see me take a piss?'

So I think the way you do it is to kneel down beside it and feel yourself into it. Then you stand up very slowly, maintaining your aim. If you're making a noise, you're winning – you certainly don't waggle it about all over the place. You get back into the bed and if it's wet – you've missed. If you get into bed and *she's* wet – you've *really* missed.

One punter was told by his mates that if he wanted a good time with his wife, he should cover his willy up with clotted cream, little chips of hazelnut on top, a little chocolate sauce and a big cocktail cherry and then get his wife to lick it all off. Off he goes to the supermarket, buys all the stuff and goes home. Next day he comes into the factory and his mates ask how it went.

'Did she enjoy it then, eh?'

'Well,' he says, 'by the time I'd put a' that cream and hazelnuts and chocolate sauce an' that cherry on ma willy, it looked so bloody tasty that I ate it masel!'

Two wee boys sitting in a train compartment with an old lady. One of them goes:

'It's spelt W-W-O-O-M-M-B-B.'

'Naw,' says the other one. 'It's spelt W-W-O-O-O-O-M-M-M-B.'
'Actually,' says the old lady, who's been listening to them. 'It's spelled W-O-M-B.'

'What d'ye mean?' says the first wee boy. 'I bet you've never even seen a hippopotamus, far less heard one fart under water!'

Farting. I've always thought that was a case of bad design. I mean, if God had meant you to fart, he would have given you a funnel. Because, in every other way, the body is perfect. At least, mine is.

It would have been much better if you could fart with your fingers. Then if you're embarrassed, you just put your hand out the window . . . or up the lum . . . or in the wain's trousers. You're having tea with someone and you feel it coming, just stick your hand out of the window. You could hardly do that with your bum! Especially in Glasgow – someone would throw darts at it.

And the human race being so inventive, someone would probably put wee flutes at the end of their fingers and play a tune. You could hardly do that with your bum.

But I think farting's psychological. Like if you're in the desert, a thousand miles from the nearest person – you never fart. You can go around doing all the things they do in the desert all day – nothing. Eat beans all the time if you like – nothing. But as soon as you're back from the desert, meet a bit of stuff, it's 'Hullo—' THUURT!

She takes you back to meet her mother. It's the whole number: the Standard lamp, the wee dog by the fireside, the chocolate biscuits wrapped in silver paper. You go in to meet her and it's –

'Hullo, Mrs Mc—' THUURT!

And I don't care if you've got nineteen A-levels and you're a brain surgeon with NASA, she will always remember you as the guy who farted the first time he walked in the door.

You're at the cinema. First date with a wee bit of stuff. First date ever, you know the feeling . . . trying all the wrong doors at the cinema and the big commissionaire inside grinning all over his face . . . Up to the balcony and you're sitting down.

'Would ye like some sweeties? No? An ice cream, then?...
Very good film, eh? Mmmm... oh, sorry! Ma hand
slipped – I was tryin' tae see ma watch...'

And then you feel it coming... BRRRRAAAAMMMM...
starting right up in your Adam's apple. And it's coming
right down through your body. It's going to be a
CRACKER! And you're looking up and saying:

'Why *me*? Why me? Why no' dae it tae the guy beside me?
He's married – his wife wouldnae care!'

It's coming down now, it's getting near. And there's nothing
you can do about it. For one very simple reason – your bum
can't suck. So you have to find a way to get out of your seat.

'Oh, will ye look at that? I'm right oot o' fags. I'll just go
and get some now...'

'But you don't smoke.'
'I'm going tae start.'

Trying to walk up the aisle with your bum shut. It's like a
cooking apple! And people are trying to help you – they
think there's something wrong with you. Into the lavvie,
into a cubicle, lock the door and let it rip –
TTHHHHHHUUUUUUUUUUURRRRRRRRRR-
TTTTTTTTTTTT!!!! Bouncing off the walls like a
balloon with the air let out of it...

I've always wondered: the Queen. I wonder, eh? I bet if
she does, it goes 'Poop'. Probably does it with her pinkie
out; it'll be something they teach at finishing school. One
thing: I guarantee she doesn't say 'Good arse' when she's
done it! 'Pretty little botty,' more likely.

Two lumberjacks out in the forest, chatting away like lumberjacks do:

'How's your trees?'
'Oh, fine thanks . . . I just got a new tartan shirt.'
'Oh, very good . . .'

And they get round to talking about the coldest places that they've ever been . . .

'Oh, I've been in some cold places, so I have. One place I was in was cold, cold, cold, cold, *cold*. Aye, it was that cold.'

'Well,' says the other one, 'I was in one place where it was *so cold* that when you took a piss, the piss would freeze and you would have to snap it off from your willy!'

'That's nothing,' says the other lumberjack. 'I was in one place that was so cold that when I woke up at night there was this little block of ice in bed beside me. Didn't know what it was. So I took it to the fire and heated it . . . and it went THUURT!'

A friend of mine called Jimmy Copeland, an actor, told me this one and he swears it's true. So if it's not, you can blame him, not me.

He was in London acting in one of those awful English plays, you've seen it a hundred times:

'You can come out now, Inspector, I think you've heard enough.'

'Yes – enough to put you behind bars for the rest of your life!'

Anyway, Jimmy was in this play that had been running for six months. He was playing the part of the villain and he had that scene when the hero comes in . . . the hero's this good-looking young bloke, who's all windswept and interesting, and who's always called Steve. Now Steve's girlfriend has been murdered and Steve's been working on his own – not with the police – to track down the murderer.

So you get to the scene when Steve bursts in on the villain, Jimmy, who's a businessman. And Jimmy's sitting behind a desk in his office, smoking a cigar. In comes Steve.

'You did it! You killed Cynthia!'
'Oh? What makes you think that?'
'I found her blood-stained semmit in your wardrobe!'
'Oh . . . that's very clever of you . . .'

And Jimmy reaches into the drawer of the desk and pulls out a gun and shoots Steve.

Well, they've been doing this play for six months and it's boring the arse off them. So one night, before the show starts, the guy who's playing Steve takes the gun out of Jimmy's drawer without him knowing and hides it. Comes to their scene . . .

'You killed Cynthia!'
'Oh? What makes . . .'
'I found her . . .'
'Oh . . . that's very . . .'

And he's reaching into the drawer – nothing! Tries the other drawers – nothing. Starts to panic.

Then his Glasgow upbringing comes to the rescue. He leaps out from behind the desk and puts the boot in, kicks Steve right in the balls. THHHOOOMP!

Down goes Steve, moaning and groaning away, on the floor. And, to his eternal credit, he remembers he's in a play and lifts himself up from the floor, sighs:

'The boot . . . was . . . poisoned . . .'
And collapses.

HECKLERS

The great problem with hecklers is that quite often you just can't hear what they're trying to say to you, especially in the Apollo, Glasgow, because they're all so far away. All you can hear on stage is a sort of 'Giewabeennarrrack'. So of course I shout back something rude and then find out afterwards that all they were trying to say was: 'Just keep goin', Big Yin – ye're magic.'

Some ripostes . . .

(To noisy, aggressive hecklers):
'Last time I saw a mouth like yours, pal, Lester Piggott was sitting behind it.'

*

'The more I hear of you, the more I believe in birth control.'

*

'If you're sitting next tae her – dae us a favour: put the heid in.'

*

'Just keep talkin' so's the bouncers can find ye . . .on ye go, Igor – kill!'

*

'Away and bite yer arse.'

*

'If you're in the next seat, put a net over her, will ye?'

*

(To quiet, verging-on-the-silent audiences): 'Aye . . . we may be poor, but, by Christ, we're miserable.'

*

'To an artiste, applause is like a banquet. Thanks for the cheese sandwich.'

*

'You're a great crowd . . . what's wrang wi' ye? Got yer balaclavas on back tae front?'

*

(When tuning up):
'Aye . . . just tae think that when Mozart was my age, he'd been deid for seventeen years.'

*

'I just washed ma hair – cannae dae a thing wi' the sink.'

*

(To heckler in London shouting for a performance of the Crucifixion – 'Gi'e us the Crucifixion, Big Yin!'):
'Aye . . . gi'e us three nails and I'll show ye.'

*

(To persistent heckler in Liverpool, while Tory Party Conference is on in Blackpool):
'You should be in Blackpool, pal. They're talkin' shit there, too.'

*

(To shrill woman, shrieking):
'Never gi'e yer mother a free ticket . . . she was even on at me tae put on clean underpants in case I was in an accident . . . You know, I used tae believe when I was a kid that if I had clean underpants on, nothin' could touch me . . . I would walk across busy streets in Partick, absolutely sure that I was safe . . . *Now*, will ye shut up?'

*

(To noisy hecklers in Dublin):
'Hey, put the house lights on. I want tae *see* an Irish joke.'

*

'Does the Mother Superior know ye're out?'

*

(To photographer taking flash photo):
'Take as many as ye want. It doesnae worry me – I used tae be a welder.'

*

(Sudden giggle in the audience):
'Unexpected laugh – always check your fly.'

*

(To loud noise of heckler being thrown out in Manchester):
'Someone just brought him a telegram frae his auntie – it said "GTF."'

Epilogue 1

In the *Evening News* review of Billy's first night in London, he was hailed as a 'Superstar' . . .

'Sadly,' the review went on, 'Connolly is destined to become a millionaire, world-wide super-star. He'll probably end up with a season at Las Vegas, a TV series and a lost sense of humour.'

No chance.

Epilogue 2

Goodnight, my dear, and sweet repose.
Lie on your back, and you won't squash your nose.

Glossary

Agley Squint
Arra Are the, as in 'We arra peepil'
Assa That's the, as in 'assa gemme'
Awrright All right. Usually a form of greeting, as in 'Awrright, eh, pal?'
Balloon Idiot, foolish person, dolt
Bears Aggressive, often inebriated, men
Bevvy Drink. *Bevvyed* Drunk
Blootered Drunk
Brek Break, as in 'Gi'es a brek'
Broo Social Security, the Social Security office
Bung Tip, bonus
Bungaroo See *bung*
Carry-oot A carrier bag containing drinks, usually bought in an off-licence
Chanty Chamber-pot
China Friend, chum
Didnae Did not
Dooni Down the, as in 'dooni hill'
Dug Dog
Dumpling See *balloon*. Sometimes has connotations regarding physical shape of person, i.e. fattish, rotund
Eejit Idiot
Fly-man Smart, often unscrupulous person
Frae From
Gauny Going to
Gemme Game, as in 'assa gemme'

Gi'es Give us
Greet, to To cry
GTF Lit. – Get to fuck, a form of abuse
Hame Home
Heavy Scottish beer, the equivalent of 'bitter'
Also a wild, aggressive person; a brawler
Kent Knew
Laldie As in 'gi'e it laldie'; maximize the effort, play hard
and energetically. Originated from name of Italian
composer, Giovanni Laldi, whose work was much requested
Lug Ear
Lum Chimney
Lumber Young women
Ma My, or mother, as in 'ma ma'
Magic Excellent, terrific, outstanding
Murder-polis A cry of alarm, an expression of extreme
concern
Nae bother No problem
Ned Young thug
Peepil People, as in 'we arra peepil'
Pluke Spot, blemish
Polis Police
Punter Lit. a gambling man; also fellow, a customer
Ruby Murray Curry
Shitehouse Lavatory
Shout on Hughie Be sick, vomit. Taken onomatopoeically
from 'Huughhheeee!'
Snotter Nasal effluence, matter from the nose
Spark Electrician
Stoatter Big one, fine person, large person, darling,
imposing person
Tore into Get deeply involved in, sate oneself with
Tube Unintelligent person
Wain Child
Wheech Get rid of

Willy Male organ
Willy-watcher Person who shows unusual interest in another person's male organ, usually in public convenience
Windae Window
Yer Your
Yin One

Tom Sharpe
Riotous Assembly 35p

Riotously funny, savage and shocking

In *Riotous Assembly* anything can happen . . . and everything does!

A crime of passion committed with a multi-barrelled elephant gun . . .
A drunken bishop attacked by a pack of alsatians in a swimming pool . . .
Transvestite variations in a distinguished lady's rubber-furnished bedroom . . .
Famous battles re-enacted by five hundred schizophrenic Zulus and an equal number of (equally mad) whites.

'Crackling, spitting, murderously funny' DAILY TELEGRAPH

'Savagely hilarious' SUNDAY MIRROR

'Does what *Catch 22* did . . . outstanding' BOOKS AND BOOKMEN

Indecent Exposure 60p

The brilliant follow-up to *Riotous Assembly* . . .

'Explosively funny, fiendishly inventive' SUNDAY TIMES

'A lusty and delightfully lunatic fantasy' SUNDAY EXPRESS

'All good, dirty fun' DAILY TELEGRAPH

Lewis Grassic Gibbon
Sunset Song 70p

Chris Guthrie knew love and hate in the same breath.

Hate for the ceaseless toil of a life in the Mearns that brought her mother to tragic despair . . .

Love for the tumbling land of her heritage – a love shared by Ewan, with whom she finds ecstatic union . . .

Cloud Howe 60p

Married again, now to Robert Colquhoun, minister, Chris sets out on a new life with new hopes . . .

As industrial strife and class struggle bring violence and discontent to the lively, bustling community of Segget, so Fate brings devastating changes to her life.

Grey Granite 60p

Living in a new world of factories, pubs, strikes, marches, riots, tanner hops, picture-houses and picketl ines, Chris's hopes for the future lie in the burning love between her son Ewan and Ellen Johns – a love as tempestuous as the times . . .

Selected bestsellers

☐ **Eagle in the Sky** Wilbur Smith 60p
☐ **Gone with the Wind** Margaret Mitchell £1·50
☐ **Jaws** Peter Benchley 70p
☐ **The Tower** Richard Martin Stern 60p
(filmed as *The Towering Inferno*)
☐ **Mandingo** Kyle Onstott 75p
☐ **Alive: The Story of the Andes Survivors** (illus)
Piers Paul Read 75p
☐ **Tinker Tailor Soldier Spy** John le Carré 75p
☐ **East of Eden** John Steinbeck 75p
☐ **The Adventures of Sherlock Holmes**
Sir Arthur Conan Doyle 75p
☐ **Nicholas and Alexandra** (illus) Robert K. Massie £1·25
☐ **Knock Down** Dick Francis 60p
☐ **Penmarric** Susan Howatch 95p
☐ **Cashelmara** Susan Howatch 95p
☐ **The Poseidon Adventure** Paul Gallico 70p
☐ **Flashman** George MacDonald Fraser 70p
☐ **Airport** Arthur Hailey 80p
☐ **Onward Virgin Soldiers** Leslie Thomas 70p
☐ **The Doctor's Quick Weight Loss Diet** Stillman and Baker 60p
☐ **Vet in Harness** James Herriot 60p

All these books are available at your bookshop or newsagent;
or can be obtained direct from the publisher
Just tick the titles you want and fill in the form below
Prices quoted are applicable in UK

Pan Books Cavaye Place London SW10 9PG
Send purchase price plus 15p for the first book and 5p for each
additional book, to allow for postage and packing

Name (block letters)————————————————————

Address————————————————————————

————————————————————————————

While every effort is made to keep prices low, it is sometimes
necessary to increase prices at short notice. Pan Books reserve the
right to show on covers new retail prices which may differ from
those advertised in the text or elsewhere.